The Digital Wilderness:

A Guide to Internet Dating

S.L. Chernik

The Digital Wilderness:
A Guide to Internet Dating
Copyright © 2017 by S.L. Chernik

No part of this publication may be
reproduced, distributed, or transmitted
in any form or by any means, including
photocopying, recording, or other electronic
or mechanical methods, without the
prior written permission of the author,
except in the case of brief quotations
embodied in critical reviews and certain
other non-commercial uses permitted by
copyright law.

Tellwell Talent
www.tellwell.ca

ISBN
978-1-77302-683-1 (Paperback)
978-1-77302-685-5 (eBook)

Acknowledgments

This book would not have been possible without the encouragement and support of family and friends. In particular I would like to thank: Tania Gee (initial editing), Ewa Defasio, Donna Cucheran, Suzanne Harris (writing coach) and my mother, father, sister and brother for their help and belief in me.

Dedication

To all those looking for love, may your search bear fruit (or at least give you some good experiences and good stories to tell).

Contents

Intro

Going into the wilderness can be one of the most enjoyable and rewarding experiences of life, but it is important to be properly prepared, know about the dangers, and choose your trails wisely in order to get the most out of the experience with the level of risk that's right for you. The digital world of Internet dating has a lot of similarities—both in terms of the potential of finding great beauty and joy, and the risk of running into predators and pitfalls. In the real world, just taking the time to get good shoes and bring water can make a hike both safer and more enjoyable, and when going online to find love there are similar small steps that can improve the overall adventure. This guide was written to try to help fellow travellers learn from the experiences of others with tips, advice, anecdotes and friendly warnings to make the trip a little smoother, a little safer, and hopefully a bit more enjoyable overall. *(Throughout this book you will find anecdotes from interviews with actual Internet daters, with their ages in brackets, although their names have been changed to protect their privacy.)*

Before You Internet Date

CHAPTER 1

It's Hard to Fish Successfully in a Tiny Pond!

The truth for many, especially once we leave school, is that it can be really hard to meet new people, particularly single people who are also looking for someone to date. It is even harder to find the few that really catch our attention and interest.

My journey into Intent dating started with a combination of frustration with the in-person options at my disposal, frustration at my lack of a dating history, the desire to try something to change my fate, and a little bit of advertising and finally some encouragement and advice from friends and family. I worked in a mostly female office. I had a short walk to work on which I didn't meet people very often. My hobbies were either female-dominated, or if men were present, they were usually already part of a couple or were gay. While I occasionally attend Christmas and Easter church services, overall I'm not a practising religious person. I have a diverse friend group, with greatly varying schedules, so getting together to go to a bar or club was difficult. It didn't help that I'm enough of an introvert to struggle with those options as venues for meeting people anyway!

I wanted love in my life, so I'll admit to it: the eHarmony and match.com advertising looked convincing. Internet dating was no longer brand-new, nor a joke, nor relegated to a small segment of the population, so even family and friends advised giving it a try. It all led to me thinking, "Why not?" and I took the plunge.

Since that time, I've noticed that many of the people I've spoken with, both men and women, often mention very similar factors when asked what influenced their decision to try Internet dating.

To help you make your decision as to whether or not the "larger pond" of Internet dating is right for you, let's take a closer look at the factors that influence people to make this choice. Let's start with looking at more "traditional" options potential daters have for finding romantic partners, aside from the Internet.

» "Meet Markets"

(Yes, Meet Markets, not "Meat Markets." The spelling of this heading is meant to acknowledge that many who choose to Internet date are truly looking to "meet" their life's romantic partner, not just find a one-night stand.)

While bars and clubs still exist, outside of cities like London or New York that have a strong "pub culture" or "bar/club culture," going to the local pub, bar or club as the typical way to spend an evening isn't as common after university, college or trade school, severely limiting the potential pool of adults who you can meet at such venues.

The general level of sound in many clubs can also limit how well you can get to know someone you meet there, unless both of you are fluent in sign language!

An additional challenge of relying on venues such as clubs and pubs, is that many people simply don't enjoy bar culture, particularly "hooking up" (a.k.a. one-night stands), as a way to meet serious boyfriends or girlfriends, and even those who once did often don't enjoy it as much as they used to as they get older. It is difficult for anyone to find a serious relationship if only one person in the pair is interested in more than a single night of fun.

Safety concerns can also make it difficult to focus on being open to new relationships forged in bars. Women in particular receive multitudes of warnings throughout their lives about how dangerous it is to go to a bar or a club alone: the need to watch out for their drinks being drugged, the potential for them to be harassed or attacked, etc. This is why many women would never consider going to a bars or a club by themselves—and with friends often having different work schedules and responsibilities, it can make it difficult to coordinate a night out.

Going to bars in groups can also make it difficult to take the first step. It is intimidating to introduce yourself to a stranger you are attracted to. This act can be even harder why you try to do it in front of ten of their—or your—friends. It's difficult to present yourself in your best light if you are worried about how you look or sound to others.

» Religious Functions

Meeting romantic partners at church or religious functions works for some people but such events generally represent very small pools of potential dates—or these pools are simply inaccessible to those who either: aren't religious, or are comfortable with the idea of romance with someone who does not share their particular religious beliefs. Being willing to date someone of a different religion by meeting them at a church function is like being willing to go for a hike in the Yukon when you live in Nova Scotia and lack the travel funds to get there. It's well-intentioned but ultimately extremely difficult to achieve!

» Social Circles

Once you are over twenty-four years old, and have been living in the same place for five to ten years, odds are you have already dated everyone in your social circle that you would be remotely interested in dating—or there is simply no one in your social circle who is eligible to date. This is particularly true if you are a divorcee or widow/widower, or have just gotten out of a long-term relationship. Most likely the majority of your social circle is made up of couples, not singles, and everyone has some opinion about the divorce or death of your former partner. It is likely you want a truly fresh start, and to do this you need to get out and meet new people. You haven't tried to meet new people in a long time, however, so where do you even begin?

» Workplaces

The perils of workplace dating are widely known; however, as in my case, even if you're willing to take your chances, the opportunity for a workplace relationship might not even exist. Many industries are either mostly female or male-dominated, so, if you are heterosexual, opportunities to interact with members of the opposite sex can be rare. The same with smaller companies or situations where people work from home—you just might not be exposed to potential relationships in your day-to-day work environment. If you are homosexual or trans, workplace romances can carry even greater risks—either of being outed or, depending on your country and its laws and culture, being fired, denied promotions/references, etc. In worst-case scenarios, LTGBQ employees can even face physical or verbal attacks or jail time.

» Hobbies, Sports & Leisure Activities

Hobbies can also be a problem, depending, of course on what your hobbies are and your sexual orientation. Certain styles of dance such as all female ballet or belly dance classes or non-co-ed sports (such as all-male or all female hockey, basketball or football teams), give people little opportunity to meet someone of the opposite sex. For the LGTBQ community, the culture/predominant attitude of some sports or hobbies may make it difficult to openly pursue same-sex romantic relationships with teammates, classmates, etc. As previously mentioned, the LGTBQ community tends to face greater risks when making romantic passes than the straight community, making it more difficult to strike up romantic relationships through hobbies.

Compounding the issue is the fact that very few of us have the time, money or energy to take up hobbies. Pretending interest in a hobby you don't actually enjoy, just for the purpose of meeting potential dates, forces you to wear a mask—pretending to be someone you are not and thereby reducing your chances of finding someone attracted to the real you.

» Meeting through Routine Activities

The final killer to our chances of finding our perfect mate in our day-to-day lives is routine. Once we graduate, and particularly once we find a job, our lives tend to fall into patterns: we see the same friends, shop at the same places on the same days, work out at the same times at the same gym, or walk our dogs along the same routes at the same times of day. The result is that the pool of new people we meet shrinks to encompass only those whose routines coincide with our own. The potential love of your life could live just down the street but if you go to work and return home at different times, shop for your groceries at different stores and have different hobbies, you may never have the opportunity to meet! You are left completely unaware of their existence, just as they are unaware of yours.

The first serious relationship I found online typified this situation: we were both from the same city, had attended the same university, had even taken some of the same courses (in different semesters) and our parents only lived a ten-minute drive from one another but we both had to move cities and try Internet dating in order to meet!

» Feel Weird About It? Why?
Internet Dating Is Just Like Online Job Searching

Will you get mocked for Internet dating? Maybe, especially if you are surrounded by negative or judgmental people, or people who are afraid to try and want to build themselves up by tearing your attempts down. Other people might light-heartedly tease you about going online to find love, but depending on your mood and perspective it can be demoralizing to be the brunt of other people's jokes. There may even be times you feel down, depressed, frustrated or angry about "having" to go online to find love or feel that you have somehow failed because you haven't met your soul mate in the "old-fashioned," in-person way. Be kind to yourself: you haven't failed, and negative people are always going to find something bad to say about everything. You are doing something proactive: not waiting around for the perfect person to ride by on a white horse and rescue you from your tower. Let's face it—if Mr. or Miss Right showed up on your doorstep one day out of the blue, in this day and age most of us would find it pretty creepy and close the door in his or her face, concerned about how he or she got our address or sceptical about what he or she was trying to sell us.

Internet dating is a pro-active way to say that you are actively interested in, and are looking to find, a relationship. The best comparison for online dating sites is on-line resume sites like

Monster.ca or Jobshop.ca. The perfect job for you might be out there, but to have even a chance of finding it you need a decent place and way to start looking.

There is no shame in posting your resume online when looking for a job, and so there should be no shame in posting a dating profile online when looking for a relationship. Much like with a job search, however, the key to success is doing some research and spending enough time and attention preparing both your profile and yourself so that you have the best chance of catching the attention of the kind of person you actually want to meet.

Just like with job searches, the odds are you probably aren't going to find the person of your dreams right away. You are most likely going to find several candidates who come close to what you are looking for—individuals who have some but not all of the characteristics you want in an "ideal partner." You will be faced with the choice of going out on dates with these candidates or rejecting them outright. If you reject them, you then have to choose to either leave your profile up as it is, or edit it in an effort to attract the person or type of person you are really looking for.

> *"One of my roommates mocked me for Internet dating but within a couple of months he had broken up with his girlfriend and had no dates while I was going on at least one a week. He stopped laughing." – Sam (28)*

» Right Mindset

It is important to know why you are looking for someone. Why do you want a romantic partner in your life? Are you looking for companionship? A lover? A helpmate around the house? Someone to fix your life or someone to give you a life? Someone to show off to your friends, parents and/or ex? A storybook romance?

How much do you want this person in your life? Are you willing to deal with inconvenience to find them? Are you willing to deal with the inconvenience they will bring into your life? (Being on your own is often far simpler than being in a relationship, especially when it comes to coordinating schedules!)

Your mindset, personal beliefs and motivations will strongly influence your results and your willingness to spend the time and effort it will take to Internet date, or even to date at all. It is worth stopping to think these things through before starting to use the Internet as a tool to meet people and attract potential dates.

» Beware the Power of Belief

While some degree of filtering is crucial for your own mental safety, it is also possible to be your own worst enemy in the search for love. For example, if you believe that there are no good men/women out there, or you believe that there is no one who is right for you. Or if you go in with the attitude that Internet dating is stupid and isn't going to work anyway. Guess what, the odds are you will prove what you believe!

The behaviour that accompanies these types of beliefs is the rapid rejection of literally every profile you read: "Too ugly, too pretty, too old, too tall, not tall enough, doesn't make enough money, makes too much money," etc., etc., etc.

» The Profile Picture and The Other Side of the Coin. Determining What You Want in a Match

Sections of this book go over this topic in detail, but if you are looking for excuses to reject people, you can always find them. Don't blame Internet dating if your mindset prevents you from finding anyone who you would even be willing to have coffee/ tea with!

If you view going online to look for love as a sign of desperation, a chore, a pain, or as something that is not worth your time or your energy, you are setting yourself up for failure. You won't put in the time and energy to research properly, to prepare your profile properly, or follow through and actually take the time to really read others' profiles and go through all the photos posted. You need to know why you want to be in a relationship and why you want to use the Internet as a means to meet people in order to have the motivation to follow through.

» Being Single

There is nothing wrong with being single. Nothing. If you are enjoying your life as a single person you are not a freak, a weirdo or somehow defective. You are not stuck in romantic limbo, waiting for your "real life" to begin. You are a complete human being living a complete life who happens not to have a romantic partner. Your intrinsic value does not come from being in a relationship. Nor does it depend on the "enviable" qualities of your romantic partner (wealth, important career, good looks, etc.) when, and if, you do find one.

You may, in fact, not even want to seek a romantic partner right now, particularly if you are devoted to your career or other work that you want to give all your time to. Many people who accomplished great things—Nikolas Tesla, Jane Austen, Oprah Winfrey, Leonardo da Vinci, Queen Elizabeth I, Sir Isaac Newton, President James Buchanan, Louisa May Alcott, Florence Nightingale, Clara Barton, Diane Keaton, Susan B. Anthony, Orville and Wilbur Wright, Greta Garbo, Franz Kafka, Ludwig van Beethoven, Harper Lee, Bill Maher, Coco Chanel, Wilt Chamberlain, Sheryl Crow, Henry David Thoreau, Al Pacino, Linda Ronstadt and Jeremy Wade, just to name a few—never got married, yet led/continue to lead interesting and full lives.

If this works for you, great! It's your life, live it in the way you want and need to.

It is actually more respectful to you and any potential romantic partners to be realistic about the amount of time and energy you are willing to devote to a relationship; if you don't have enough time to date, or taking on one more thing will just make you miserable, then wait until you actually have the time/want to spend the time looking for love.

Don't try Internet dating to find a steady relationship if you enjoy being single just because someone else or "society" thinks you should be in a relationship. Doing so will betray who you truly are and will betray whomever you date, as you will be reducing the time they could be with someone who actually wants to date them.

> *"Try not. Either do or do not. There is no try."*
> *Yoda, Star Wars Episode V: The Empire Strikes Back*

» What if I Am Older?

As early as 2011 one of the most interesting aspects of the Internet dating phenomenon was that there seemed to be more people aged 40 plus on online dating sites than those under 35, and it was more common to hear stories of relationship success from the older crowd. While this may have to do with the fact that more people in their twenties and thirties can be uncomfortable admitting that they met online (although this is diminishing as time goes by), it appears that, generally, more people aged thirty-five and older are willing to give Internet dating a try.

This may be a result of time-crunched lifestyles where the obligations of kids/family and careers have left people with little time to meet new people so they turn to the Internet for help. The point here is: Don't be intimidated or hesitant about joining an Internet dating site just because you are over a certain age!

The numbers may be changing however, as evidenced by this 2014 *Global News* piece:

> **Users**[1]: 100 million worldwide for PlentyOfFish, with four million active every month.
>
> **Single Canadians:** 14.2 million in 2014, according to Statistics Canada.
>
> **Online dating:** A 2011 Leger Marketing survey found 36 per cent of Canadians between the ages of 18 and 34 use online dating.
>
> **Growth:** Six per cent per year for online dating and related services in Canada since 2010, according to research firm IBISWorld.
>
> **Mobile:** Sixty per cent of online daters in the United States were using only mobile devices as of July 2014, up 25 per cent from the year before according to research firm ComScore. The combined mobile audience of the Match Group and PlentyOfFish was 10.9 million.
>
> **Millennials:** Fifty-three per cent of dating app Tinder's audience is between 18 and 24. The mobile app has grown to be the third-most popular in the United States since launching in September 2012."

Does this mean that older daters should stay away from Internet dating? Not at all. Internet dating should never be looked at a guaranteed way to find love, just one more place to look. So regardless if you are over or under 35, if Internet dating is something you are open to then it is worth giving a try.

» A Cautionary Note

If you are older, however, you do need to think very carefully about the age range you are willing to date. Most people seem to be the most comfortable dating within a five- to ten-year span of their own age. When there is a difference of fifteen years or more, many people start to feel uncomfortable about this, and the greater the span, the greater the risk of discomfort. If you are looking to date a much younger man or woman keep in mind that this will limit the pool of people who will respond to your profile. Also keep in mind that even a successful "May-December" relationship is likely to be judged, often negatively, by others. If you are comfortable with this, great! Carry on. If not, then set your profile to only search for matches within five to ten years of your own age.

» On the Flip Side

If you are a younger person who is honestly attracted to and wants to date people who are fifteen or more years older than you are, be very careful how you set your preferred-match age range on the profile. It can be very disconcerting for someone (particularly when they are in their twenties or thirties) to view a potential match's profile and realize that the preferred age range indicated is so broad that it includes both themselves and their parents! When setting an age range, start by setting a five- to ten-year range, confining your search to the age group that you believe interests you most. If this doesn't work out then feel free to increase the range.

> *"One woman emailed me, and her profile looked pretty good at first, then I noticed that her preferred age range was wide enough to incorporate both me and my dad who was divorced and also Internet dating at the time. The uncomfortable thought that we could both end up*

going on dates with the same girl was enough for me to delete that profile from my list of matches." – Sam (28)

"I was the next man!" – Indiana Jones, Indiana Jones and the Last Crusade

» Age Ranges and the Question of Kids

If you are a younger person looking to date someone fifteen or more years your senior, keep in mind that the older person in the relationship may already have children from a past relationship and may have no desire to have more with you—or you may be the same age as his or her children. If having children who are biologically your own, or having any children at all, is very important to you, make certain to be honest with your match; if he or she doesn't share your desire then he or she probably isn't the right person for you.

If you are the same age as your match's children, make certain you are comfortable with this, and be prepared for the fact that the children may not accept/be comfortable with your romantic involvement with their parent.

» Regardless of Age: If Your Match Has Children from a Previous Relationship

Please keep in mind that you are not someone else's child's parent unless you are formally asked to be, and you might not have a full grasp of the family history/dynamics of the relationship between your match (the parent) and his or her kids. Tread carefully and cautiously—don't ever try to "fix" the relationship between a parent and his or her children, or impose your ideas on discipline, eating habits, etc. on the kids. Respect the parent, his or her rules, and how he or she is choosing to raise his or her kids, but use this information to determine whether or not you could be in a long-term, committed, relationship with this person. If the children are in their late teens or adults, tread particularly cautiously—they will make their own choices as to whether or not to accept you and/or your help on their own time. Respect their choices!

» The Distance Question

Many Internet dating sites will ask you to specify a geographical boundary for the search/matching function of the site such as: anywhere in the world, in the same country, in the same province, or in the same city. It sounds very romantic to say you are willing to search to the ends of the earth to find the person who is right for you, but practicality rears its head really fast. If you did meet someone online who sounded like a really promising and interesting match but that person lived in Australia (while you live in Canada), would you prepared to swallow the expense of meeting him or her in person, or would you expect that he or she would be the one to travel all the way to meet you? Even splitting the distance and meeting in the middle (i.e. Hawaii) is not cheap. Would you be willing to do this for someone you had only met online?

It is hard enough to try long-distance dating if you have met the person and know that there is a connection between you—a connection that both people are interested in trying to preserve and strengthen despite the miles between you. Even when you have met in person, long-distance dating rarely works unless both partners put an enormous amount of effort into the relationship. Be honest with yourself with respect to how much time, effort and money you are willing to commit to a potential long-distance relationship.

When you meet someone online, keep in the back of your mind all the stories you have heard of people claiming to be a twenty-year model when they are in fact fifty years old, weigh four hundred pounds and are married, and try to maintain a healthy level of scepticism. If it sounds too good to be true, it likely is—but not always. Meeting someone in person is a great way to be sure that he or she has not been lying about anything major (such as age, height, weight, occupation, etc.) online. The closer you set the distance perimeter on your search/matching questionnaire, the more likely it is that you will have the opportunity to actually meet the person and move your relationship from online to real time.

For more info on the darker sides of internet dating, and behaviours to watch out for, please take a look at "From Ghosting to Kitten Fishing, a Guide to Modern Dating Terms" by Liz Conner, Sept. 18, 2017, which can be found online at Standard.co.uk .

If you live in a country that is desirable as a location to immigrate to, such as Canada, be cautious about matches with individuals in countries where many people wish to emigrate from. There are some individuals who view marriage as the fastest way out of these countries and who may see you more as a potential entry visa than a love match (Maplematch.com is an online site for Americans looking to date Canadians that has become fairly popular since President Trump was inaugurated).

Not everyone is like this, however, so don't assume that everyone has ulterior motives; just be cautious. If you set your preferred distance broad enough to include matches from other countries, it is something to be aware of as you start pursuing a potential relationship online.

Take the time to be aware of why you feel the need to set your search to a wide distance. Self-esteem can affect the distance you perceive you need to find someone who would be attracted to you. Starting with a distance range the size of a province or a territory rather than a city can be a sign that you feel you are undesirable. So undesirable, in fact, that you have to search that large of an area to have any hope of finding someone who would be attracted to you. This is a flag that you probably need to work through some of your own issues before trying to date, because it is very hard to successfully attract someone else if you don't believe that you are desirable and don't value yourself.

I had this problem the very first time I tried Internet dating. Having been asked on an extremely low number of dates in my life, part of me honestly believed the odds of finding love in my own city were very low. So I set the distance parameters to encompass two provinces. This meant, of course, that it included many small towns that I had no interest or even ability to move to, since my career essentially requires I live in at least a mid-sized urban centre. The unexpected—and undesirable—result of this setting? I was hit with so many suggested matches that searching through them was an exhausting and frustrating process, especially since most of them lived in locations that were incompatible with my reality. The ones who did interest me? Well, it was extremely difficult to meet in person due to the travel involved, and when we did make the effort there usually wasn't a single spark of chemistry between us.

On the flip side, setting broad distance parameters could be a reflection of your reality—if you are a forest ranger working in the middle of nowhere you might have to set your range to at least 100 to 300 kilometres (62–186 miles) in order to actually find someone to date.

» Different Motivations? No Problem

The motivation that drives people to try Internet dating is going to vary radically from person to person—some do it on a whim, some do it because they really want to find "the one" and others give it a try because they are curious as to just who might be out there/who they would be matched with. Some might be looking for love for the second time after a divorce or the death of a spouse, while others want a way to find a match without subjecting themselves to the inevitable scrutiny of singles events—or the risk of running into their ex!

"I tried Internet dating for a couple of reasons. I hadn't had a lot of success with 'traditional dating' and my time in university was rapidly drawing to a close. Looking around I realized that soon I wouldn't be among a large group of peers and finding like-minded people to date was going to become even more difficult once I graduated, as I would have a diminishing number of social contacts. It was also a sort of experiment—I wanted to prove to my friends that normal, reasonable people were online and were using this medium to find each other." – Gordon (25)

"I had been in a long-term romantic relationship that ended about six months before I started Internet dating. One of my friends had met her husband through Internet dating so she encouraged me to try. I was watching TV and saw the eHarmony commercial and thought 'Why not?'" – Eliza (31)

"My divorced father had started Internet dating and originally I signed up on the site as kind of a joke and a way to check up on what he was doing; only after I started getting messaged did I start to take it seriously." – Sam (28)

Be warned; if you don't treat Internet dating seriously and act like it is just a joke, then your results will probably reflect this attitude. If you decide to look for love online, do yourself a favour and choose to put some real effort into it — don't act like a teenager who is too cool to care. If you just slap something together and throw it up on the site then guess what? That is how the world will see you. Your profile is literally the only thing that potential matches have on which to base their impression of you. Since that profile is what the world is going to use to judge you as a potentially desirable mate or not, why not make the best first impression that you can?

» Body Image

One of my professors at university did a lot of work in Central and Latin America and he told us an interesting story about the perception of beauty. His wife was very, very good-looking by North American standards but every time she accompanied him on his work trips, the men in the villages he was working in would shake their heads and say to him, "You poor man to be saddled with such a skinny, ugly wife. Don't worry, we'll fatten her up while she is here, then she won't be so ugly."

North American/ Western society is not kind with regards to body image, particularly towards women, and has become pretty notorious for its limited depictions of beauty. Over and over again, Western media tells us that we have to look a certain way to attract a guy. The reality is that this is not true. Different people are going to find different physical features attractive or not, and as in the story above, different cultures have very different ideals of beauty.

There is an excellent movie called *Phat Girls*, which turns the North American idea of beauty on its head when three American women attend a conference for Nigerian doctors and experience a different standard of beauty. One of the pivotal scenes in the movie is when the main character realizes that she had found a guy who loved her for exactly the plus-sized woman she was; however, since she couldn't accept herself as she was, she was unable to believe that the relationship could succeed. We have to be careful not to be our own worst enemies in terms of letting our own biases and assumptions about what is and what isn't attractive undermine our chances of finding love.

There are guys and girls out there who appreciate large women, just as there are guys and girls who appreciate tall women, petite women, skinny women, etc. The same holds true for men and women who are attracted to men; some are attracted to tall guys, some to short, some to hairy, some to bald, to skinny and some to buff. A large part of being desirable is truly believing, or at least accepting, that you are/will be desirable to the right person for you!

If you are uncomfortable with your body, try to find a physical hobby that makes you feel good about yourself and confident in your body shape and size. Try to track down episodes of shows like *What Not to Wear* and *How to Look Good Naked* (specifically the British version, not the North American one, since the British version was better) for advice on how to dress to best flatter your own body type, and to see how much we can create distorted perceptions in our own minds of what we actually look like. Go out and find some form of physical exercise that builds up your confidence in yourself and in your body, so that when you meet someone new you present yourself as comfortable with who you are and what you have to offer in the physical aspect of your relationship. Learn to love or at least accept your body, to feel at peace inside your own skin, regardless of whether you fit society's stereotypes or not. Look for advice on sites like SensualitySecrets.com on how to flirt in a classy, confident way, regardless of your body type. If you need it, seek professional help such as therapy, hypnotherapy, and/or self-love coaching to work through any body image issues you may have.

Plastic surgery is an option but unless you are correcting an issue that is causing you physical pain or is affecting your health (i.e. breast-reduction surgery) this should only be an option of last resort. If you don't feel like a complete, worthwhile person, changing what you look like on the outside is not going to solve the problem. If you actually like yourself, then the decision to go on a diet or get plastic surgery can be made from a place of strength. You are not choosing to diet or get surgery because someone else wants you to, or to impress someone else, you are choosing it for yourself, because you are already in a good place and want to make your life even better. If you do go through with it, take the time to do your research, find a good surgeon and opt for the more natural version of any enhancement, so that the end result matches your body's proportions and won't cause any additional health complications, such as strained neck and back muscles, etc.

Women should also watch old Mae West movies or YouTube clips. She is a great example of a woman who is perfectly comfortable with her femininity and with her intelligence. She is extremely sexy in a classy way, and her body language is worth studying for the way it conveys her sexual confidence. Not all of us can pull off her brashness, but all of us can learn from the way she carries herself and the way she moves.

When looking to increase body confidence and express sensuality, both men and women can also try something daring like taking a burlesque class. Pushing your boundaries in a supportive environment can help you find your version of sexy. If the idea of a class is too intimidating, you can watch burlesque videos on YouTube. Burlesque Hall of Fame videos can be found on YouTube under the title BHOF with a year number (i.e. BHOF13—Burlesque Hall of Fame 2013 videos). A great documentary on the subject is Immodesty Blaize's *Burlesque Undressed* for those who want to know more about the history of burlesque and what sets it apart from stripping (a.k.a. peeling).

For me, the thing that helped most with my body confidence was *danse orientale*, a.k.a. belly dance. I have always done dance of one sort or another and had always found the idea of belly dance interesting, even though I didn't know much about it. I wanted to get more in touch with my sensual side in an effort to help me feel more confident and sexy so I decided to sign up. I tried a couple of classes and found an instructor whose style I really liked (Donna Cucheran, who currently teaches several dance belly dance classes at the Bedouin Beats Studio in Edmonton). Her classes were open to women of all ages, shapes and sizes. Even though real belly dance isn't what I thought it was based on what I knew from the movies, these classes were like therapy for my body and my brain. Between my classes and the performances, I saw women from size zero to size twenty-plus, and from age nineteen to age sixty-plus dance together and dance beautifully. These ladies proved that size, shape and age had little effect on grace or style. Over and over I saw what real women looked like when they exposed their stomachs, instead of the ubiquitous airbrushed, photo-shopped maga-zine models, which helped to reset my internal perspective of beauty and body image. Attending these classes reassured me and gave me comfort that even though I'm not 5"10 and I weigh more than 100 pounds, I could still be happy and confident with my body, and that I could be proud of how I looked and how I could move. Real belly dance isn't about seducing men as Hollywood would have us believe; it is about learning how to be a confident female, comfortable in her own skin, who can move her entire body with control and grace. It is about learning to be powerfully feminine. This confidence was the real the lesson I needed to learn.

» Deal Breakers

To borrow a phrase from Doctor Phil, there are acceptable reasons to break off a committed relationship: for instance, if your date/boyfriend/girlfriend/partner/spouse violates one of your "deal breakers." Deal breakers are the things that you are completely unwilling to compromise on—someone doing these things destroys the trust in the relationship to the point it cannot be repaired (at least from your point of view). Before you start Internet dating it is a good idea to have a really clear idea of what your personal deal breakers are at this point in your life.

Common deal breakers include alcohol or drug abuse, cheating, stealing, and physical, verbal or emotional violence/abuse (including overly controlling behaviours/extreme jealousy, etc.). Each person in a couple will have his or her own deal breakers, as only they can determine what is important enough to constitute one. For one person a deal breaker could be the lack of a proposal after three years of dating, while for someone else it could be the lack of a proposal after ten years of dating.

Deal breakers are the things you hold sacred, the things that you are absolutely not willing to give on, so choose them carefully, and slowly make your significant other aware of what they are. Then if your significant other violates one of your deal breakers then you will be faced with the choice to stay in the relationship or not. If something was important enough to you to be a deal breaker, then violation of this should be reason enough to break off the relationship. Make certain the other person understands that he or she has committed one of your deal breakers, and either explain that is why you are letting him or her go, or, if you want to give the other person a chance, ask him or her to cease and desist and provide a time frame, if possible. If they fail to comply with your request, then it is up to you to do what you need to do, which usually means walking away. Having deal breakers means you have standards. If the other person isn't willing to respect your standards, do you really want to be with him or her for the rest of your life?

In my last relationship I had to face the reality of having personal standards and deal breakers. One of my standards is that I will date guys who are divorced but I will not date guys who are newly separated. Personally, I think it is bad karma to mess with anyone's marriage and in the eyes of the law a separated couple is still technically married. When I began dating this individual I was under the impression he was divorced, but I found out after two months that he was simply separated and had not even filed for divorce yet, despite the separation being "amicable." I had to weigh the fact that he had been a good date for those two months against the fact that continuing a relationship with him would violate the standards I had for myself. In my eyes he wasn't free to pursue a relationship with me, and I did not feel right staying in a relationship with him. I let him know that if and when he ever did get divorced, if I was still single then I would be interested in going out again but not until then.

He didn't get it, not even a little bit, as he saw his previous relationship as over despite his legal status. His arguments as to why he thought we should continue dating showed me our values had far less in common than my initial impression, making me far less inclined to date him ever again.

While giving in and resuming our relationship would have been the easy thing to do, it wasn't the right thing for me to do. I had to hold to this belief even as some of my friends told me I was crazy for holding to my standards. Thankfully, my family and one of my friends supported my decision, but the lack of support from many people I respected was hard to take.

As an aside, in an odd twist of fate, after a few months this individual actually thanked me for holding on to my standards.

My unwillingness to compromise on something important to me helped motivate him to truly get on with the process of separation and now he and a mutual friend are happily dating. I'm happy for both of them as they truly suit each other at this point in their lives.

This situation served as a great lesson to me about what it really means to have standards. Standards don't mean a thing if you aren't willing to uphold them, even if it means that the relationship you are currently in might end and people might judge you for making that choice. Did the relationship ending hurt? Yes. Am I happier now and proud that I am not still in that relationship? Absolutely, as it wouldn't have been good for either of us in the long run and both my former boyfriend and our mutual friend would have missed out on meeting each other in the right way for them.

On a serious note, please keep in mind that in Internet dating, deal-breaking behaviour is often not exhibited in the initial online stage; it can take five or more dates, or the change from Internet dating to in-person dating for a partner to start exhibiting these traits. Sometimes this behaviour won't show itself in day-to-day interaction, but will come out in out-of-the ordinary situations such as vacations. For example, someone who doesn't normally drink much goes to an all-inclusive resort in another country and suddenly a whole other side to them comes out; one that disturbs and scares you.

In other words, it's like dealing with a predator with really good camouflage, who looks and acts in a way that is very attractive at first until their prey is in a vulnerable situation and then the predator's real nature comes out. It is important to remember that these people do exist and to always have an exit strategy (e.g. don't go on a trip with anyone unless you can afford to make it home on your own if need be).

If someone starts acting in a way that puts you in potential danger, you need to get as far away from him or her as possible, as soon as possible. Block them from every method of communication, report them to the dating site if you are still online, and if necessary, talk to the police about restraining orders. Remember that you owe such an individual nothing at all, no matter if he or she was "nice" at first, if she or he paid for anything (dinner, the vacation, etc.), or if he or she told you they loved you/that you made them behave this way—*do not* let anyone guilt trap you into staying in the relationship. *Fifty Shades of Grey*-type behaviour is abusive, not romantic behaviour (and FYI, it completely lacks the consent element so critical in the real BDSM community). It's important to know the difference (especially since abuse and unhealthy relationships are often marketed as "romance"). No one, no matter his or her lifestyle, sexuality, etc. deserves to be abused. Ever.

An Overview of the Day-to-Day Reality

Most likely, the majority of us of age to be Internet dating have seen the old eHarmony commercial with the perfectly matched couples describing the instant connection they felt with each other. It is a brilliant marketing campaign—the problem is it promised a reality that is rarely experienced among those who try Internet dating. Internet dating is almost never like a fairy tale where people have a Cinderella moment and fall in love at first sight within the first month of signing up to a site. If you expect instant results or to feel immediately connected to the first person with whom you are matched, you will inevitably be disappointed.

When I first tried Internet dating I experienced a problem I never expected. I went on a date with someone who was rated as a 95 per cent perfect match for me according to the site. The problem was, when I went out with this person we found we had absolutely nothing to talk about! It turned into half an hour of awkwardly looking at each other, desperately attempting to keep some sort of conversation going, and finding that every topic fizzled after two minutes. What made it particularly hard was that I had left the house with such high expectations and yet nothing about the date made me want to repeat the experience.

One of the most important things to accept is that Internet matchmaking services, twenty-seven parameters of compatibility or not, are not a perfect judge of who is going to be the right person for you. Some people can be too similar, to the point where both of you of you have the same opinion about absolutely everything, while other people can be so different that you can't find common ground, despite the fact you have similar values. You may like the same things, such as certain TV shows, but for completely opposing reasons. Some people are just not going to be right for you, and it can sometimes be hard to pin down why that is; you just know it in your gut. Well, here are four words to remember: ALWAYS TRUST YOUR GUT.

Internet matchmaking services are simply a good signpost, indicating where the odds of a probable match are highest, but they are not a commandment from on high, declaring that any one person is *the* perfect match for you. You will still need your own judgment to determine whether or not you want to pursue any relationship, and you hold the responsibility for how the relationship turns out, not the dating site.

When you try Internet dating, expect that some days are going to be exciting; some days will make you angry and frustrated; while on other days, checking profiles and email messages will just feel like another chore. It is critical to keep a positive attitude and take each day as it comes, otherwise you will become so burnt out by the process that you will sabotage your chances of finding the right person for you.

In the next couple of chapters I will break down the realities of Internet dating: how the sites work and what it like to go on dates, as well as things to keep in mind if you do progress past the online stage.

» When Overabundance Has the Potential to Be a Bad Thing

With Internet dating one of the biggest problems can be switching from encountering too few potential matches to encountering far too many. Thousands of people have Internet dating profiles, and if you don't find ways to filter out some of the people you are not looking for, you will become overwhelmed and fatigued long before you can find the person who might be the right match for you. Think long and hard about what kind of person you are really looking for, and try to target your search as much as possible to improve your odds of meeting that person!

If you are serious about finding a relationship online, it should not be a popularity contest where the goal is to see how many people you can attract. It should be about trying to attract the right person for you—and you only need to find one. It is much easier to decide what flavour you want at an ice cream parlour that offers a choice of ten flavours (all of which you like) than at one that offers a choice of fifty (especially if you have to sift through forty-nine of them you don't even like to find the one you do!) Do yourself a favour and only look to find the best potential matches for you.

» The Differences between the Sites

Much like the various online resume sites, the various dating sites offer very different features and formats, price points and options. Sites like eHarmony promise to do matchmaking work for you while sites like PlentyOfFish (POF) just give you a place to put up a picture with a quick summary of yourself and what you are looking for. EHarmony is one of the most expensive sites, while POF is one of the cheapest.

Based on casual conversations I've had with people the most commonly utilized sites, (aside from Tinder, which is still perceived as more geared a little more towards the one-night-stand crowd), seem to be PlentyOfFish, Lavalife, Match.com, Chemistry.com and eHarmony, but there are many others out there, including JDate (the Jewish dating site) and BBW (Big Beautiful Women) for those of larger size and those who wish to date women of larger size, and ChristianMingle for single Christians. The number of niche sites such as JDate appears to be growing, so take the time to research whether or not there is a niche site for you. Niche sites can help target your search while general sites like Match or eHarmony can expose you to a larger pool of potential dates. There are great summaries on the Internet detailing the strengths and weaknesses of the various sites that are worth taking a look at before you decide which site to go with. Top10bestdatingsites.ca rates EliteSingles, Match and ourtime.com as the best sites in Canada, but individual experiences with each vary according to the individual reviews.

One of the most important things to know is that the different sites have different rules regarding who can post a profile. For example eHarmony will let divorcees sign up but it won't post the profiles of those who are separated but not divorced, while POF has no rules regarding who posts. Knowing ahead of time who can post on the site can save you over an hour of filling out questionnaires only to discover on the last question that the site won't let you post your profile anyway.

> *"I used OKCupid, a site I heard about from a friend. It was a free site, which asked you to fill out a whole series of random questions from serious (i.e. How many kids do you want?) to silly. It also asked you to rate how important each question was to you and they used your answers and the degree of importance you placed*

on each answer to suggest matches for you. The more quizzes you filled out, the better the odds were of the site matching you with someone who really suited you, and there were even quizzes that members could suggest, anything from your favourite Star Trek character to your dating history, and it was possible to see other peoples' scores. Although it was a relatively new site at the time, the interface worked well and was easy to use. Overall it worked pretty well but I especially liked the fact that it was free." – Gordon (25)

» **Who Is on the Sites?**

People of every age, occupation, religious background, and race are on Internet dating sites, from every country in the world. Blue-collar workers, white-collar workers, entrepreneurs, minimum-wage workers and millionaires—you name it, you can probably find it. In addition, the membership of the sites is in constant flux, with new members joining while other members leave as their subscriptions run out or they find successful matches.

The key point here is the first time you try Internet dating you might not find anyone you are interested in, BUT THAT IS OKAY. Take a break for a month or two then try again; the right person for you may have posted a profile in the meantime. Alternatively, try switching sites, as you may find that the people on one site are a better match for you than those on another or you might prefer the format of one site over another.

This happened to me. I signed up for a year-long membership with eHarmony and was sent plenty of matches, but despite the site's best efforts I just didn't feel enough of a connection to pursue any of them beyond a couple of dates. I was getting tired and frustrated so I made a plan: when my membership ran out I would take a break for a few months and try going to more singles events. Then, once I had recharged a little, I would try again but maybe on a different site. The second time I signed up I tried Match.com and within a couple of months, I'd met a better match for me.

When that relationship ended after a couple of years, I found myself starting at the beginning once again. This time, when I went to sign up for Internet dating I chose to go with Match.com again and decided to also give Chemistry.com a try.

Don't be afraid to sign up on more than one site or give different sites a try to see which one suits you the best.

» Price

Price is a tricky subject when it comes to dating sites. In general, the price of the site can serve as a filter regarding the types of people who will sign up to use it.

In a classic example of you get what you pay for, I noticed that on the free or least expensive sites many of the profiles (in my age range, at least) are geared toward finding hook-ups rather than potentially long-term, monogamous relationships. Other profiles on the free sites were clearly jokes. On the more costly sites, however, the dominant characteristic of site members seems to be the desire to find a relationship that could become long-term. Many of the high-end, expensive sites don't even offer the option to indicate that you are searching for a short-term fling.

Some people I talked to told me that the free (or very cheap) sites were more trouble than they were worth, as they got message after message from people they had no interest in and some of the messages were wildly inappropriate (i.e. one woman told me that she was shocked when she got an invitation to join a sexual threesome on PlentyOfFish. Other people on that site, and on Craigslist, have told me that they have been sent multiple pictures of genitalia without their consent/any requests for such images, to the point they got tired of even checking their messages!).

Free sites offer the most choices for the least cost, but the time and energy needed to weed out the good from the bad may be more of an investment than you want to make. This is not to say that people can't find great, long-term, monogamous matches on the free sites, just that you may have to filter through many more profiles to find them!

> *"Some buddies of mine liked to create joke profiles on POF (PlentyOfFish) and send them to friends just to mess with them, since it was free and only took a couple of minutes to do." – Sam (28)*

» Time

The time it takes to register for any Internet dating site can be thought of as another form of cost. The eHarmony questionnaire takes 1 to 3 hours to complete, while it takes about 45 minutes to get set up on Match.com and on POF it can takes as little as fifteen minutes.

Time can also come into play when you consider how long it takes to start conversing with or meeting your matches in person. It seems fairly common for people who are registered on both eHarmony and Match.com to report that they were already dating their matches on Match.com in the same amount of time it took them to just begin email conversations on eHarmony.

» Safety

It is important to keep in mind that when sites are free or have few or no barriers to posting profiles it is far easier for Internet bottom feeders (predators, con men/women, people pretending to be someone they are not) to use them. The more time, effort and financial cost involved and the less likely it is that bottom-feeder types will bother, particularly when there are so many free sites out there. That being said, keep in mind that there is no guarantee that the people on the expensive sites aren't bottom feeders, either. Take steps to protect yourself such as only using your first name or a username, and never giving out your address, your landline phone number (if you have one) or your exact place of work until you have had at least a couple of (in-person) dates. When you go on dates, tell someone that you are going on one, where you are going and when you expect to be back, especially the first time. Make certain the location is public like a restaurant or a mall, not a house, apartment, garage or isolated country road, hiking trail, lake, or any place where you'll be all alone.

> *"If you are walking down the street one night and you think there is someone lurking behind the building, you are paranoid. If you are walking down the street and you think there is no one behind the building, you are stupid. If you are walking down that street and think there MAY be someone hiding behind the building, you are intelligent!"*
> *– Brad Schultz, Quantum Health Newsletter*

In 2017 a very sad news story came out of Calgary, Canada, where a woman met an Internet date in person for the first time at a hotel and ended up being held hostage and abused by him (sexually assaulted, burnt,etc). Be careful of hotels - meeting in a restaurant in one is likely okay for a first meeting, but if you do choose to accompany someone to a private room make doubly certain to have an emergency contact and let them know where you are and what to do if they don't hear from you by a certain time. This is just like a hiker letting someone know they are going hiking, so if they suffer an accident or an attack people know where to start looking, who they were with, etc. If you have taken reasonable precautions and something bad does still happen (as it might), please keep in mind that even the most prepared and careful outdoor enthusiasts can still get hurt or die in the wilderness if something goes wrong. In other words, what happened to you wasn't your fault, and please come forward and get the help you need to recover.

» Doesn't Everyone Lie Online?

When Internet dating it is like you are dealing with a credibility credit card. At first you have to assume people are telling you the truth about themselves, because if you assume that everything they post is a lie, why would you want to meet them? In other words, the statements they make in their profile and their answers to site questionnaires are like purchases on a credit card. The first couple of meetings are like when the credit card comes due—if they were truthful in their profile they will have no problem paying off their credibility credit card—all their physical characteristics, age, occupation, etc. will match what they wrote in their profile and emails. When this happens, their credibility rating goes up and they become a "preferred customer," someone you are more likely to go on a second or third date with.

If they sort of match—are within a couple of years of what they said, are close to the physical type they specified and are at least in a related industry to what they stated as their occupation, they may not be a preferred customer, but they may be worth giving the benefit of the doubt and one more date. If nothing matches, then they are in credibility debt and aren't a good investment for any more of your time or attention—walk away and don't look back.

To put it another way, imagine the pleasant surprise of meeting someone who said he or she was fifty online and finding out they actually are fifty years old! You feel respected since the person didn't lie to you, and are more likely to consider him or her to be worth a second or third date. If this is what you want in a potential Internet date match, take a stand and be truthful in your own profile.

» An Avalanche Waiting to Happen

Avalanches are caused when rain or melting temperatures followed by a quick freeze create an unstable "shelf" upon which snow accumulates. The more snow, the heavier the pressure on the shelf, until the whole thing collapses with little warning.

Lies when Internet dating work much the same way; they may not seem like a big deal at first but the first one creates an unstable shelf. Generally, lies require further lies to be kept up over time, putting more and more pressure on you and your shelf. If the weight gets too heavy, the shelf may break and then the snow pack of lies will come plunging down. Odds are the impact will crush or suffocate the romantic relationship the same way real world avalanches crush and suffocate those unlucky enough to be buried under them. Occasionally someone is saved from this fate and survives the experience, but most outdoor enthusiasts know better than to count on this degree of luck.

In other words, when thinking about whether or not you want to be truthful in your Internet dating profile, it can also be helpful to think about the amount of effort involved in keeping up such a persona, or mask. If you state in your profile that you are adventurous and love skydiving, guess what? The person you attract will likely want to go skydiving with you and the choices you will be faced with then aren't going to be pretty. You can fess up and admit you've been lying all along, or you can keep lying, which means you will have the weight of one more lie on you, and you will likely have to jump out of a plane!

If you lie to attract a partner at the outset of the relationship (no matter how minor the deception), you will be expected to maintain it for the rest of your life unless you confess your lie at some point. How exhausting does that sound? And would you every truly trust someone who had lied to you in order to get you to fall in love with him or her?

You should never try to be what someone else wants you to be. You want to attract someone who will love you for being you—not for being something you are not. Every lie you put in your profile is one more barrier between yourself and your potential perfect match, making it less and less likely he or she will ever find you. Don't sabotage your own search by sticking a persona between you and your potential dates!

» Profile Lies and Safety

Since safety is a major concern with Internet dating, the credibility credit card is very valuable. It is a short leap in people's mind from a lack of credibility to the idea that you represent a potential threat to them (i.e. you may be a con man, a stalker, an Internet predator, etc.). By keeping your credibility rating up it increases your chances of success.

In order to protect yourself, pay attention to your match's credibility rating and whether or not it goes up or down the longer you interact with them. Check in with your gut; if you start to feel uneasy/uncertain about a person, trust yourself! Get out and don't look back.

» Sending Money

Never send money to someone you have only met online or have only met a time or two in person, especially if he or she lives in a foreign country. It does not matter how good someone's story is or how desperate he or she sounds. Just don't do it! This is how most Internet dating scandals work, so always err on the side of caution and make it a personal rule not to do this under any circumstances.

» Plan Ahead for Success

Take into consideration what might happen if everything goes well. What if you meet the love of your life, the perfect person for you, and he or she lives in another province, state or country? Would you be willing to leave your current job and move your whole life somewhere else? Would you expect the other person to do that for you? Be brutally honest with yourself regarding your expectations and options. Does the nature of your career allow you to work in another town, city, province, state or country? Are you expecting your partner to financially support you, making the question of whether or not you would be able to work where he or she lives irrelevant? Set your distance parameters to match the reality of your life, your values, and your plans for your future.

The nature of my day job makes it extremely difficult for me to move anywhere without changing jobs, so for me, it makes more sense to look for matches in my immediate area rather than all across my province or country.

CHAPTER 3

A Matter of Attraction

» Writing a Profile

Writing an Internet dating profile is much like writing a cover letter for your resume. You are trying to sum up, in a page or less, who you are and why you should be considered for the post of boyfriend/girlfriend. An added complication is that you are also like a prospective employer, trying to sum up in a page or less what you are looking for in a potential boyfriend/girlfriend.

The trick here is that you are not writing this resume just to a person's logical, rational mind. You are also writing to reach his or her heart! You want to attract them by engaging their emotional side rather than convince them through just their rational mind to be interested in you. You can't tell someone you are a "great catch" and have him or her believe you—you have to show them why they would want you in their life. You are literally painting a picture with your words of how great their life will be with you in it. In this way writing an Internet dating profile can also be compared to a product marketing campaign. You are the product. You need to package yourself as attractively as possible so that the person you desire to meet will also desire to meet you!

You want your profile to stand out among the hundreds of profiles on the site and catch people's attention, but you want to catch it for the right reasons. You don't want to come across as arrogant, angry, insecure, negative, or as if you are asking for the impossible, and yet you want to show that you do have some standards and you aren't just looking to date anything that breathes. You want to convey your personality but not come off as too weird, crazy or boring—at least not to the kind of people you are attracted to!

Think really hard about the question of attraction: are you writing a profile that you would be attracted to or are you writing a profile that would attract the kind of person you are attracted to? Men and women can be and often are attracted to different things, so if a woman writes the kind of profile that would attract her it is important to know that that profile might not be attractive to a man and vice versa!

"My friends describe me as nice to be around. I like movies, going out for drinks with friends, and my dog. I value my family. I work hard at my job because I really enjoy it."

The person in this fake example sounds perfectly pleasant but nothing about this profile is memorable; a thousand other people could have one just like it. While it isn't the automatic "Click, on to the next" a negative, angry profile generates, there is very little here that urges someone to "like," "wink" or "email" the writer in order to get to know him or her better.

Keep in mind the difference between logic and attraction. Do you know anyone who is single, has a job and is a nice person but that you aren't attracted to at all? Has a friend or relative ever listed the "virtues" of a potential blind date to try to convince you to meet him or her and it hasn't made you the least bit interested in meeting that person? Remember that when writing your profile. Listing the logical, rational reasons someone should be attracted to you may not get you the results you are hoping for.

Dating isn't a contest where the most qualified candidate automatically gets the guy or the girl. In your profile think about trying to show someone why they would want to date you through the pictures you form with your words rather than simply listing off all your best attributes.

Be prepared to write several drafts of your profile—it will save you time, effort and the expense of going on bad dates later.

In case anyone finds it helpful, I've included a sample of the Internet dating profile from my last attempt at Internet dating. I would encourage you not to use it as a template or to outright plagiarize it, since it reflects me rather than you, but I offer it as a brainstorming prompt for you to write your own.

"I'm a lady who dances to the beat of a dwarven drum. Just kidding, but I am most definitely a fan of geeky things (including movies, comics and anime) so if that isn't something you would enjoy in your life, please move on and good luck in your search!

My life is very much a balance of opposites: my day job working for a union is highly analytical, but after work I'm also an entre-preneur working in a highly creative field. I enjoy people-filled events like a fancy dress ball or a taiko concert or a Comic-Con, but I'm also enough of an introvert to need some people-free time afterwards. I love long discussions about the serious aspects of the world but also about the most silly and random of things. I enjoy good food in moderation (including making said food), but I'm not really a "party animal." I like going for walks, hiking in the mountains and occasionally fishing, but I'm not a typical "outdoorsy-type" girl. I'm highly intellectual, and can get stuck too much in my head, but I'm also very sensual, with an unusual level of attention to details like colour, texture and sound. This side of me can really be seen in my hobbies of dance and cosplay

(I'm an award winning costumer at Edmonton Expo and I make most of my dance costumes.)

If this is a trivia question of what characters I am most like, I would have to say: Belle, Galadriel, Hermione, Princess Zelda and Peggy Carter.

I can be very kind and thoughtful, but in order for that well not to dry up I need someone who would enjoy being kind and thoughtful towards me, too. For instance, there are days when I really enjoy the thought of planning an evening or figuring out a gift someone else would enjoy and other days when the idea of someone else taking on the planning and arranging things without me having to ask sounds like the most romantic thing in the world! Like many kind people, however, I can be a bit stubborn about accepting other people's kindness in return, so please offer it to me with enough conviction that I know you mean it!

I'm looking for a guy to be the yang to my yin, a partner who complements me while I complement him to the point we both become greater, more complete, by being with each other. I'd like to have some, but not all, interests and hobbies in common, and enough physical and emotional attraction to go with the mental attraction to justify dating over friendship. Examples of guys who impress me most are individuals like Hugh Jackman or Tom Hiddleston—classy, with interests in many different areas, romantic, and confident enough in themselves to be willing to get on the dance floor or laugh at their own expense."

» So What Are People Generally Attracted To?

According to *Time* magazine's *The Science of Marriage* issue, 2017 *"Some elements of attraction are nearly universal and probably evolved over the millennia to help us identify healthy mating partners. We tend to gravitate towards people who look robust, with clear skin and bright eyes (clues to potential fertility). Most of us are interested in people who come from backgrounds similar to our own, and who have the same ballpark level of attractiveness and education. And cleanliness is a surprisingly strong aspect of attraction across cultures. A happy demeanour helps too. Several years ago, Swiss researchers found that people rate pictures of the same face as more attractive when smiling than when he or she has a neutral expression—and a joyful beam was enough to make the raters judge even relatively unattractive people favourably."*

The article goes on to also include factors such as smell (we tend to be attracted to those whose subtle smell indicates they have a very different major histocompatibility complex—a different arrangement of genes involved in immune functions—than ourselves, which is thought to promote more robust immune responses in offspring among a species).

According to *Time* magazine's *The Science of Marriage* issue, 2017: when it comes to attraction, our own mental "love maps" that we've built over a lifetime of exposure to love and attraction ideals in our own family, society and culture, as well as our personal experiences with friends and former relationships, are just as important as physical characteristics. These mental maps grow and change as they are refined over time, but may influence why some people find the "bad boy" attractive, while others prefer the "good dad" archetype or the "girl next door" versus the "femme fatale."

Of particular interest to those who are Internet dating, the Time article referenced above mentions that in 2015, Australian researchers found that "when looking at online dating profiles and describing their ideal partners, both men and women preferred non-conformists, meaning those whose clothes, opinions or life decisions broke the norm. Being different can be extremely attractive. And it makes sense from an evolutionary perspective, because it helps preserve diversity in the species."

For Men:

Scientific literature[2] and psychological research shows that men and women are each attracted to a specific series of traits (the exact mix of traits differs between the sexes). According to Dr. Sabongui, as per his interview in the *Sensuality Secrets* instructional DVDs:

"Most men seemed to be most attracted to women who possess a specific mix of traits. Physical/sexual appeal is important and men seem to be drawn to a woman's appearance at first. In particular, [most] men seem to be drawn to a feminine and polished appearance both in dress and body language—to her 'look' even more than her looks. Feminine does not necessary equal frills and ruffles; it means wearing clothing that is tailored to drape attractively on the body, emphasizing a woman's feminine assets. 'Polished' means that it is clear the woman values herself enough to put effort into taking care of her physical self. In this context 'polished' is the opposite of 'frumpy' or 'has let herself go.' Attraction to her 'look,' however, may only make a man want to sleep with a woman, not necessarily have a long-term relationship with her."

Fun playfulness or joking between a guy and a girl is also important, according to Dr. Sabongui. In other words, none of us want to be bored by our romantic partner, or face the prospect of going through life with someone who is serious all the time and doesn't know how to have fun. Nor do we want someone who sees everything as a chore and is always complaining. Let's face it, day-to-day life can be pretty monotonous—going to work, doing chores, paying bills—there is a reason it is called the "daily grind." Someone who conveys a playful zest for life, no matter how old they are, can make any day seem a little less boring or difficult. Playfulness alone, however, seems to make a man see a woman as a "pal," a "buddy," or "friend," not a potential date. Instead she becomes just "one of the guys."

Finally, some degree of nurturing or softness also seems to be important to most men. In front of "the guys," "their coworkers" or "the world," men may feel that they need to present a strong front. Is it any wonder then that they might search for someone who will be supportive of them when they need it? Someone to whom they can show their vulnerable side to, who won't use it against them? Someone who won't mock them for their dreams of starting their own company or building their own house? Someone who won't add injury to insult on the day they don't get the big promotion or make the big sale, by saying, "I told you so," or "I told you it was foolish—what were you thinking?"

Nurturing alone, however, or nurturing in excess of physical attraction or fun playfulness turns a woman into a surrogate mother, not a date. This is especially true if the woman is actively taking care of the man by doing everything from making food for him, to providing shelter, buying his clothes, doing his chores, etc. This is a type of nurturing, but it isn't the type of nurturing most men are romantically attracted to. After all, unless they are suffering from an Oedipus complex or particular fetishes, most men are not romantically attracted to their mothers.

Take a look at your profile and your photos. Are you conveying that you possess the traits men are attracted to? Is one coming across stronger than the others, or is a reasonably balanced picture emerging? Ask a friend to read the profile and give you feedback.

Always keep in mind that a guy is looking for a woman who will enhance his life, not detract from it. Focus on the positive—both in terms what you are bringing to the relationship and in terms of what you are looking for him to bring. It is very fair to qualify your profile in a positive fashion (i.e. "for the right man you will... "). Avoid negativity in your profile such as demands ("You must"), insults (looking for a "Real Man"), and angry rants about how you have been done wrong.

» Major Turn-Offs

Don't ask him to be a fantasy man, a prince, a white knight, a hero, etc. What flesh-and-blood man can compare to a fairy tale? And what flesh-and-blood man would even want to try? This is a contest he's doomed to lose. (Also keep in mind that many real-life heroes don't think of themselves as heroes, they just do what needs to be done!)

Negativity and anger are not attractive. No one wants to be insulted or put down, especially by a stranger vying to be a romantic partner. Either find a way to frame it positively or leave it out of your profile!

Don't focus on what you don't want; it is a waste of his time. Focus on what you do!

For Women:

According to Dr. Sabongui, heterosexual women are also attracted to a mix of traits in the opposite sex, but a different mix then men. Confidence is extremely important to women. So is dependability. Deep-down, most women want someone who they can depend on not to hurt them or let them down if they put themselves in a vulnerable position—and, even more important, someone who knows (and is confident) that they can be depended on!

A wishy-washy, nervous, or completely unconfident man is conveying to women that he isn't certain if he trusts himself, which makes it very hard for a woman to trust in him. If you went to a lawyer and he or she started the conversation with "I'm not very good at this, but I'll try my best," would you hire that person? Probably not. Same for a financial advisor, mortgage broker, pilot, guide, physician, or psychologist. Each one of these people is in a position of trust where errors have the potential to cause the client financial, mental, emotional or physical pain. When determining whether to interact with anyone in a position of trust most of us are looking for confidence and skill; in the same way, women are looking for a man who gives off the impression that he knows what he is doing, so it is safe for them to put their trust in him.

To most women, a complete lack of confidence is as unappealing as overwhelming neediness is to most men. Many adult women take care of themselves: they hold their own jobs, pay for their own housing, and possibly support children. For a woman to allow a man into her life, into a position that has the potential to bring her emotional, mental, financial or physical pain, she is looking for a man who can confidently step up to the plate. (Important note: being inexperienced isn't the same as being unconfident. Inexperienced people can start off by being confident in the basic skills they do have/ their ability to learn. They then work to get better. Unconfident people do not acknowledge or make use of the skills they do have, including their ability to learn and improve. Since they don't trust they can, rather than working on learning and improving, unconfident people often seek constant reassurance that its okay they aren't as good at something as they want to be, struggle to make any decision at all, etc. Sometimes Clinical Anxiety symptoms are missed because people think these are just symptoms of a lack of confidence. In order to truly address these types of issues (clinical anxiety) seeking professional help is strongly recommended.)

Personally, I love to dance and, for me, I can really tell the difference between a man who is confident in himself as a dancer/leader and one who is not. When a confident man takes the lead his steps are sure, his frame is solid and it is easy for me as his partner to surrender to his lead—to trust him not to hurt me by stepping on my toes or running me into the couple dancing behind us. The guy might just be able to do the most basic steps, but he knows he can do the steps he does know well, and that trust in his own abilities is very clear to me as his partner. When a man without self-confidence takes the lead, his steps are uncertain and his arms are often limp as wet noodles. It is almost impossible for me to figure out what he wants to do because he himself is not certain. Because he doesn't trust himself I rapidly become convinced I can't trust him. The skill of following absolutely requires the ability to trust in your partner for the duration of the dance, so when I lose my trust in my partner, I start unconsciously trying to take over the leadership role. This results in an awkward and uncomfortable situation for my partner and me as we subtly and often unconsciously begin to fight over who is actually leading, and the fight often results in feet being stepped on. Needless to say, these situations are not ones I remember with fondness or any desire to repeat. A man doesn't have to be Fred Astaire to try to dance, or Cassanova to try to date, but trusting in himself and his abilities at least a little bit will definitely help others to see him at his best.

It is important to note that confidence isn't arrogance, however. A confident man has no need to brag about his strengths or act like a jerk. Because he isn't trying to be strong—he is strong (emotionally and mentally, not necessarily physically).

According to the research cited by Dr. Sabongui, women generally like men who have their lives together; men who are successful at making a living day-to-day, or who are, at the very least, on a path to being successful in the future. Men over the age of twenty-seven need to have a very good reason to still live with their parents or on their friend's couch. A good reason could be supporting ailing parents, saving for a mortgage, or cultural norms (living with extended family is very common in some countries, such as the Philippines). Deadbeats are not attractive dates, but someone who has love and compassion for a relative who needs their help is! Just keep in mind that most women do not want a man who can't take care of himself and is totally dependent on them in the post of their boyfriend or husband. Such an individual makes a woman feel like a mother rather than a lover, which usually kills any hope of sexual attraction.

Men need to convey to potential dates that they have their lives together in order to appeal to women. Sure you might hit a rough patch or a setback once in a while, but in many women's' mind a desirable man is someone who has a plan to work through it and get back on his feet as soon as possible. A guy who owns nothing and lives on Kraft Dinner can still be considered an attractive catch if he is putting himself through school, or saving up for a house. A man who is too lazy to shower or wash his own clothes? Not so much.

Playfulness and a zest for life are equally attractive to women as to men, for many of the same reasons. When a woman says she likes a man who can make her laugh, she is usually not talking about a comedian or a clown. She means someone who can be silly or outrageous, someone who doesn't take himself too seriously and who is willing to let her be silly and outrageous in turn. Someone who is prone to telling a woman to "Act your age," or to "Try not to embarrass me" isn't fun to be around. Neither is a man who tells a woman she should get plastic surgery, go to a gym, or "loosen up." These kinds of comments tell a woman it is neither safe nor acceptable for her to be herself in his company, and that he doesn't accept her for who she is. These comments also imply that he holds some sort of ideals as to how a woman "should be" and "should act," and that it is not acceptable for her to deviate from those ideals. This is exhausting and frustrating for a woman, as it turns her into an actress playing a role rather than someone actually living a life.

Women are attracted to men who are genuine; when a man acts one way when the two of them are alone, then totally changes his behaviour when he is around his friends, co-workers, parents, etc., a woman starts to wonder which is the real version, and usually won't bother sticking around to find out.

According to BusinessInsider.com, the following are seven qualities in men that women find attractive:

Good looks give men a "leg up" as women are more likely to choose them for short-term flings but not necessarily long-term relationships.

For long-term relationships women value selflessness over good looks.

Women may like older men as older men may have had more time to accumulate more resources (a.k.a. the "George Clooney" effect).

A sense of humour is important to women and is seen as a sign of intelligence.

Men with dogs do better with the ladies (unless the ladies are allergic)! Researchers believe it makes them seem nurturing.

In one speed-dating experiment women said they were more attracted to men who were mindful, present and non-judgmental.

Women rate men higher who take heroic and some-times primal risks like saving lives, hunting for food and playing with fire.

» Major Turn-Offs

Negativity, anger and insinuations that women are all "gold diggers," "tramps," etc.

Making your profile all about you and what you are looking for, with no mention as to what you are willing to give to a relationship or why a woman would want you in her life.

Insecurity (i.e. "I'm not good at this," or "What can you learn from a profile anyway?" etc.).

A profile that reads as a list of traits and looks like Spock wrote it as an assignment in logic.

» Clichés

Someone who makes a point of saying, "I've met the bare minimum character requirement" in a cliched way, or who fills up their profile with phrases such as "time will tell."

» Tales of Profiles

> *"In my profile I tried to create a very honest assessment (in a nutshell) of who I was. I saw a lot of profiles where people almost seemed to be trying to put on a 'face' or a 'mask' in order to attract other people, or whose profiles were so generic that I had no idea who they really were and so had no interest in contacting them. Profiles only work when people put in the time and are honest in the details they include. I went on a couple of dates where the people didn't seem to match the profile (or at least the impression I got from them online was very different than the impression I got when I met them in person) and this was very disconcerting and did not inspire any interest in continuing to date them."*
> *– Gordon (25)*

I didn't think it mattered how much detail I put down in the profile section—if we were meant to meet I thought we would anyway regardless of how much or how little was in this section. I was also worried about privacy/security—I didn't know who would be looking at the information/pictures. I did not get a lot of responses to my profile." Eliza (31)

» Security Versus Information

Security is a legitimate concern; however, the reality of Internet dating is that you have to give fate a hand by increasing the chances that something in your profile or pictures will spark the interest of the person who is right for you. The only way to do this is to take the time and put in the effort to write a detailed profile, honestly fill out all the questions on the site's forms and post multiple pictures that show the real you.

Saying you love to travel gives a general impression but there is a great deal of difference between back-country camping and staying in five-star resorts, between travelling to the next town and travelling internationally. The more specific you are and the more details you provide, the greater the chances that a reader will get a true sense of who you are and whether or not they might be a good match for you (or vice versa).

"One guy caught my interest because I was familiar with the train station that was in the background of one of his pictures—there were no markers or anything but I could tell it was taken in the country I am from. His other pictures also interested me—especially one where he was in a suit as it showed he was probably a profes- sional like me."—Eliza (31)

» Setting Your Profile Apart
by Showing Your Playful or Humorous Side

Don't be afraid to be playful and unpredictable, particularly in the sections that are considered very routine such as "occupation." After reading a hundred profiles that say "lawyer," "millwright," "engineer," etc., imagine how refreshing it would be to come across one that says: "everyday superhero to small children (a.k.a. daycare worker)," "money wrangler (a.k.a. venture capitalist)," or "detail detective (a.k.a. forensic accountant)." Writing something like this rather than just what is expected shows you have a sense of humour and sets your profile apart from the 10 to 100 other profiles a prospective match may have read that day. The site might not always allow it, but look for opportunities to put a bit of creativity and humour into whatever sections do allow for it!

Posting photos of you doing playful and unpredictable things can also work well, as it visually conveys that you have a sense of humour and can help you find someone who will appreciate that. Don't overdo it, though. If every photo is a joke, then you too will probably be seen as a joke, not as an attractive potential partner.

» The Whole Impression is Greater than
the Sum of its Parts

If the site has a "Five Things You Can't Live Without" or other values section, really think through what to list in it. People evaluate each item individually and all the items as a group.

I honestly saw a guy's profile that listed the following as the things the person couldn't live without:

1. Jesus
2. My Truck
3. Beer
4. My ATV
5. My dog/ hunting rifle

At first I wasn't sure how to take this, because it seemed to me like a movie casting for a stereotypical redneck character. The more I read over this section, however, the more I realized that if this was a true reflection of who this guy was and what he valued, great! This type of list will help you filter out matches who aren't going to fit into your world view and lifestyle.

I found such lists very helpful as a "searcher," because as soon as I saw a list like this one, I would know right away that I wasn't the right girl for that person so I could screen out that match immediately.

When Internet dating, people reading your profile have to make judgments about you and whether or not they want to date you based on your profile alone. Therefore, everything you put in your profile is of great importance: spelling mistakes in your profile lead to the conclusion you can't spell, multiple pictures of you holding alcohol makes you look like an alcoholic, pictures of you with members of the opposite sex make you look like a player, etc. So rather than just thinking about the individual parts, think about how the profile as a whole is going to look to a prospective date.

» Polarizing Statements

If you are really looking to filter out matches that don't share your interests and values, you can include in your profile interests or values that tend to polarize people into camps: those who like/share/respect the interest or value and those who do not.

Examples include rap music, country music, religious beliefs and political leanings, as well as geek references, math jokes, etc.

In my profile I specifically mention two polarizing subjects. The first is my occupation: I work for a union. In my particular part of the world there is a lot of prejudice against unions. I can't realistically be with someone (in the romantic sense) who hates my job and is unwilling to overcome his or her own prejudice. By specifically mentioning that I work union side, I am hoping that these individuals instantly screen themselves out of my search!

The second polarizing subject I mention is the fact that I like geeky things, not only because I genuinely like them but also because people usually react in one of three ways when they find that out. The first is dismissing it as a childish thing, and looking down on me for admitting the fact that as an adult I watch any form of cartoon or read comic books. This is not the kind of person I want to date! I prefer to pursue hobbies and activities that interest me even if they are not considered typical or mainstream. Someone who expects me to give up my interests to conform to their idea of "normal" or someone who requires that I always act like a "serious adult" isn't someone I want to waste my time on. I am happy if this type of person never responds to my profile; they are saving me time by filtering themselves out of my search!

The second reaction is one of accepting ignorance of the subject and general disinterest—they respect that this is one of my interests but it isn't an interest they share. They ask a few questions about it and what I like about it, but that's about it. This reaction lets me explore what our common interests are and where our interests differ; normally a person will have at least a couple of hobbies or interests that I feel the same way about (such as baseball or hockey).

The third reaction is one of great enthusiasm from people who share my interest. In this, my mentioning my geeky hobbies becomes a conversation starter. In this case, the other person's reasons for liking the same shows, comics, etc. are important clues as to how that person sees the world and what he finds funny, which are very important to me. Each reaction tells me something about that person and helps me decide whether or not I want to pursue any form of relationship with him.

Polarizing topics will cost you dates, since some people will reject you based on them, but if someone can't respect your interests and values even if they don't share them, is that someone you want in your life?

If you do use polarizing statements, be careful to limit their use to only one or two—the couple of topics that you find important to you at this point in your life. Also, be certain to make it clear that you don't expect that you and your matches will share ALL your interests—just some of them. You don't want to screen out anyone who isn't exactly like you, after all, since if you are trying to date someone who is *exactly* like you then one half of that couple is redundant.

» Get Feedback before You Post

Show or email your profile to someone (or even better, multiple people) you trust to give you good constructive feedback. They can alert you to when your tone or choice of words appears to imply something you didn't intend, such as bitterness over a past relationship or a more sexual vibe than you wanted to convey. Some phrases in the English language, for example, can have more than one meaning and while you are thinking of one, your readers might think of the other and judge you in a way you might not expect.

If you come off as bitter, most people won't want to date you. If you come off as just interested in sex, people may want to have a one-night stand with you, but many won't view you as a potential wife/husband/life partner.

If possible, show your profile to both men and women prior to posting and ask them whether or not they would consider dating someone who had that profile and if not, why not. Basically ask for their first impression of the profile and their rating of the attractiveness of the profile. This will show you if you still have work to do to create a profile that is actually attractive to the kind of person you are trying to attract.

» Spelling and Texting Abbreviations

People you trust can also alert you to spelling mistakes or grammatical errors before you post. Many people strongly dislike seeing these errors in people's profiles as it makes them wonder if the person didn't know any better, or was just too lazy or didn't care enough to correct them. Similar to resumes and cover letters, the degree of the mistake also matters—a spelling mistake like addressing a cover letter to "Dear Sir/Madman" instead of "Dear Sir/Madam" is particularly bad, as that it is the first thing the person who is reading it sees (and it makes you look as if you are trying to insult your reader). In Internet dating, a small mistake at the end of a profile might be forgiven. A mistake in the first line probably won't be.

Do not use text lingo in a dating profile unless it is specifically asked for by the site—it makes you look as if you can't spell and don't care to try. It only takes a few seconds longer to type "How are you?" versus "how r u?" or "great" versus "gr8." Remember this is the first impression you are making, so take the time to make it a good one.

» The Profile Picture

Building on the idea of being honest and confident in how you present yourself, the profile picture is the most critical part of Internet dating. Whether we like it or not most of us are visual creatures, and it is the picture that will make or break your profile. Most people who try Internet dating are very hesitant to respond to a profile that doesn't have a picture. "What are they trying to hide?" is the thought you can't get out of your head, no matter how hard you try to concentrate on the written details of the profile. Sooner or later you are going to have to meet in person, so not posting a photo also seems kind of silly to most of us. If you don't have a profile picture many people will pass your profile by, or will decline interest if you message them.

Visual images are really important in terms of attraction—they really are the first impression by which we judge the suitability of potential partner. We judge their level of confidence, their level of success and their sexual attractiveness to us by their visual appearance. True beauty is on the inside, but Internet dating it is much like going to the bar, or the coffee shop or any other public place. When you look at a crowd, certain people's appearances are going to spark an interest in you while other people will not. Without any sort of spark, there may never be any sort of fire or passion, so be cautious when responding to profiles of people whose physical appearance does nothing for you.

I made this mistake when I first started Internet dating. *Beauty and the Beast* has always been one of my favourite fairy tales, and I told myself that I shouldn't judge people by what they looked like (at all); instead, I should try to look deeper/ strictly at the profile, almost to the point of pretending the photo wasn't there at all. This approach sounded good in theory but it quickly became apparent that it would not work for me. I went on several dates where the written part of the profile looked good, or the site "matchmaker function" indicated a high percentage match of values, etc., but the picture did nothing or less than nothing for me. When I met the guy in person, it was even worse—I felt not even the smallest degree of attraction and then had to extricate myself from an awkward situation. Trust me, it is not kinder to go out with people whom you are in no way physically attracted to; you are not doing them or yourself any favours.

To be clear, a person does not need to look like a GQ or Victoria's Secret model, but something about him or her needs to appeal to you. If not, then the most you can be with that person is friends, not a romantic partner.

> *"Physical attraction is an important element of dating that can't be ignored—it may be a surface assessment but it is going to be important in the relationship on some level at least." – Gordon (25)*

When Internet dating, you are going to come face-to-face with the question of whether or not you are being shallow every time you click on a profile, but remember that physical attraction is a very personal thing, and what might seem important to others might not be to you or vice versa. Don't beat yourself up by labelling yourself as "shallow" if you are being honest about what attracts you and what doesn't. Only pursue online profiles in which the photos in which something (i.e. their smile, their eyes, their body types, etc.) physically appeals to you - otherwise you are wasting their time and your own.

It is okay to have your own standards of what you consider attractive enough to pursue and to reject matches where the person doesn't fit those standards. If you reject *every* potential match based on his or her physical appearance, however, then it is time to consider whether you are perhaps setting your standards too high, and whether or not you need to be a little more open to the possibility that a person's personality might make him or her more attractive to you.

If your definition of what is attractive reads like a lunch order—specific height, specific hair colour, specific eye colour, specific weight—then realize you aren't trying to find someone who actually exists; you are trying to custom-order a doll made to your specifications. Toss this list out and give a real, live person a chance to enter your life.

If you are not certain if you find a prospective match attractive or not (i.e. the person falls right on the line), go out on a couple of dates with the person and see if the chemistry is there or if it grows over time. If it isn't there at all, or the tiny spark dies out after two dates, the match probably isn't the best one for you.

» Photos Not to Use

Most of us have pictures that friends have taken over the years, but let's be honest: many of the pictures aren't exactly flattering. Many are of embarrassing moments such as that time that you got drunk in Vegas/at the lake/at the ski hill. Unless you are looking for a full-time party girl/guy these kinds of pictures won't get you what you are looking for.

Take a good look at your driver's licence or passport photo. Do you like or do you hate this photo? Do you feel it really represents who you are? Or is it just the representation of the most unflattering version of you?

My previous passport photo was horrible—it looked like a mugshot of an individual who is as jet-lagged as humanly possible. While it is clearly me, it is not the version of me I would want to present to the world on a daily basis. In particular, it is not a photo I would ever want to use to attempt to make a good first impression or attract someone to date me! So any photo of me that even resembled that one was not something I would ever consider using as my dating profile photo.

There is an underlying assumption in Internet dating that most people have chosen to post their best photos—to give the best first impression they can. In other words, rather than assuming that the so-so photo of you is a reflection of you on a so-so day, most people think that that is a reflection of you on a good or, possibly even your best, day! Based on this assumption, bad photos usually equal instant rejection, no matter how good the written profile looks.

"I hated profiles where I couldn't clearly see the person in the picture (too much shadow or too far away) or where you couldn't see their whole body."–Eliza (31)

It is worth spending the time and money to get at least two pictures made up: one headshot and one body shot (either a full-body photo or you can take one from your mid-calf up). You want pictures that look like you, but the best version of you. This might mean paying for a professional photographer, or at least finding a skilled amateur.

After Internet dating for a couple of months and not being satisfied with the kinds of responses I was getting to my profile, I invested in a professional photographer and found it was well worth the money. I discussed with the photographer in advance what I was looking for (pictures that still looked like me, but the best version of me) and what I wanted to use them for. In other words, I did not want Photoshopped pictures that were too good to be true, just photos with proper lighting taken from flattering angles—something the photographer was happy to help me with. Once I started using professional pictures, the number of responses to my profile greatly increased, and I now have a great set of photos of me at this age to look back on later in life.

Whatever you do, do not only use photos that you took of yourself in the bathroom mirror using your cell phone! Particularly if in the photos you are shirtless or in a bikini top!

Such photos convey that you have no friends, family or neighbours who you could ask to help, that you are too cheap to even go to the mall and find a photo booth, and that you lack the imagination to find a more interesting background for a selfie. Due to the combination of location and (lack of) attire, such photos also imply that you are self-absorbed and narcissistic—or at the very least have a highly inflated idea of your own attractiveness and are thus quite creepy! Trust me, these are not points you probably want to convey if you are looking for a quality relationship.

Only one photo that was taken by a guy of himself in his bathroom mirror ever appealed to me. In the photo the guy was dressed in a tux and it looked as if he had snapped it right before heading out to a fancy event. The context for this photo seemed reasonable—snapping a picture of yourself looking good for a formal event is something that many of us do. Taking a photo of yourself half-dressed in the bathroom mirror isn't—unless you are tracking a weight-loss or fitness journey.

» The Selfie

As selfie culture has become ubiquitous, seeing selfies as Internet dating pictures has become common. I would caution anyone, however, from relying completely on selfies as a way to market themselves. Having had the opportunity to work with really good photographers due to my hobbies, it is clear to me that photography is an art. No matter how well you think you showcase yourself in your selfie, odds are a professional or very skilled amateur can do better. If someone other than yourself takes the photo they have far more options when it comes to angles and distance from their subject than you do, even with a selfie stick. Think about it: even celebrities known for their selfies still get professional photos taken for their work portfolios, etc.

So can you use selfies? Yes. But if you really want to see yourself at your best, consider hiring a professional. You will likely be pleasantly surprised when you see yourself through someone else's eyes. (Although if you do go for professional photos, make certain to take the time to choose a photographer whose work you like and whose prices you can live with.)

» The Good, the Bad and the Blurry

I remember the first time I was scrolling through photos, I could not believe how many guys had posted photos that were blurry, in shadow, or where the photo was more unflattering than most passport or driver's licence shots! To make the situation worse, these were the main profile shots and/or the only photo included with the profile. My first thought was, "You've got to be kidding me. Really? You expect me to click on your profile and read the written portion when this is my first impression of you?"

Don't insult prospective dates by posting photos in which we can't see you. If you don't want to post a photo, then take a stand and don't put one up (although this is not recommended, either). If you are going to include photos in your profile, take the time and put in the effort to do it properly, unless your goal is to annoy and turn off potential matches.

It is critical to walk the talk when posting photos. If you don't like bad photos, photos where you can't see the person, shirtless/bikini photos taken in the bathroom—don't post any to your own profile. It is not appropriate to judge potential matches by one standard and then not apply that same standard to yourself.

Don't forget yours is not the only photo on the site! Remember how Internet dating can be compared to a product marketing campaign? On one level, you are competing for a potential date's attention with every other profile on the dating site, and everyone who views your profile will be comparing your photo with that of every other photo they have seen. If others on the site have posted professional, attractive photos and you haven't, how well are you going to compare? Don't sabotage yourself this way.

» Tips for Photos

Here are some general tips for photos, particularly the main profile photo.

For Women:

Use a photo of you!!! (never use one of someone else. People **do not** forgive this deception!)

Remember that you want whoever is seeing the photo to be able to recognize you if you were to meet at a coffee shop or a restaurant.

Don't have your face/ body partially or completely obscured by shadows in any shot you post, and don't post blurry photos—there is no point in posting these since they just annoy potential matches!

Use a photo that was taken in the last two to three years (particularly if you are between the ages of seventeen and thirty, or have experienced a major weight or muscle loss/gain).

In addition to the face and full-body photos, post a variety of shots showing you doing activities you enjoy (skiing, dancing, dressing up for Halloween, acting, reading a book, painting, skydiving, etc.) for a grand total of three to seven photos.

For your main photo, find an outfit that makes you smile when you wear it because you feel confident in it and like the way it looks on you.

Beware "tents" and "disco balls": make sure that your clothing and jewelry doesn't overwhelm you with masses of fabric or over-the-top ornamentation. You want to convey your face and body shape as realistically as possible without too many distractions.

Make sure your photo conveys your personal style, in addition to emphasizing your good features, rather than just "hiding" your flaws.

If you dye your hair, your main picture should match your current shade. If you change your hair colour/style often, post photos of you with several different looks.

Make sure that your outfit leaves something to the imagination. Think about Christmas presents: they are exciting partially because of the mystery of what they might contain. If the present is already unwrapped, then the mystery is gone. (Unless you are a full-time nudist, of course.)

Beware of clothing, such as leopard-print, or gothic garb, or uniforms such as military, police or Firefighters, that has certain connotations associated with it (e.g."cougar."). That being said, if you are part of a particular group or sub-culture, the clothing you wear in your photo can help attract others who are part of this group or who are attracted to members of this group!

Beware of clothing that is styled identically to clothing specifically made for children (i.e. T-shirts with cutesy animals, knee- length overalls with primary-coloured T-shirts, lunch boxes with cartoon characters, etc.). Children are not sexual beings and wearing this kind of clothing subconsciously associates you with children, conveying that you are not to be considered sexually desirable by any healthy, emotionally mature adult!

Beware of clothing and hairstyles that convey "frumpy" or "old," as neither is attractive. The former conveys that you have given up hope of finding a romantic partner while the latter conveys that you are past the age of finding one. When wearing clothing that suits them, even ninety-year-olds can dress in an attractive way!

If you wear makeup, try a few practice styles before you choose what you want for your photos, or if you are not confident in your skills, have it professionally done. You want to look like you, so unless you are goth/emo, or a member of Cirque du Soleil, save the super dramatic makeup for another time.

Never post a picture or send a potential match a picture of your naked breasts or genitals! No matter how proud you are of the way you look!

*Unless you have a child, don't post pictures of you holding children, particularly babies! (People **will** assume they are yours.)*

Don't post pictures of you with guys around your age unless they are clearly captioned, and are preferably relatives (i.e. "My brother and me, Christmas 2016).

Don't post pictures of yourself with multiple guys in the shot unless there is a really good explanation (i.e. you are an actor and you clearly identify the shot was from a play, you are on a coed sports team, or you are a paramedic, firefighter or police officer, etc.).

Don't post pictures of you with your ex, even (especially) if the ex is blurred/cropped out.

Don't post multiple pictures of you in a bar holding alcohol or dancing on table tops (even one can be more than enough).

If you specify that you don't drink or smoke in your profile, don't post a picture in which you are drinking or smoking—it instantly destroys your credibility rating.

Unless you have a pet, don't post pictures of yourself with any kind of pet (people with allergies screen these out immediately, and if they don't know will assume it is yours).

Profile pictures are not mugshots or passport photos—**smile**, or at least look like you are thinking about something happy!

For Men:

Use a photo of you!!! (**never** use one of someone else. People **do not** forgive this deception!)

Remember that you want whoever is seeing the photo to be able to recognize you if you were to meet at a coffee shop or a restaurant.

Don't have your face/ body partially or completely obscured by shadows in any shot you post, and don't post blurry photos—there is no point in posting these since they just annoy potential matches!

Use a photo that was taken in the last two to three years (particularly if you are between the ages of seventeen and thirty, or have experienced a major weight or muscle loss/gain).

Post photos in which you look successful (by your own definition) in life. Usually this means thinking of ZZ Top's "Sharp Dressed Man." Even if you work in a trade, take the time to get a photo of you cleaned up and looking your best.

Don't post shots of you standing in a field against mountains, etc. where all you can make out is that there is a human in the field but not much else, unless you have already posted a good face and body shot and you want to show that you like hiking, skiing, snowboarding, snowmobiling, etc.

Do not post a shot of yourself shirtless unless the context of the picture is clear and reasonable (i.e. you standing in surf shorts beside a surfboard or you playing a game of shirts and skins pick-up basketball).

Never post a picture or send a potential match a picture of your penis, no matter how proud you are of it!

Beware of clothing such as goth/emo garb, combat/hunting fatigues or uniforms (firefighter, police, military) that have certain connotations associated with them. Make sure that your outfits are conveying the image you want to convey (that said, if you are part of a sub-culture, or a member of the military or the police, etc., such clothing can help you attract others who are also members or who are attracted to members of these groups).

Make sure your photo conveys your personal style, in addition to emphasizing your good features.

If you dye your hair, your main picture should match your current shade. Same if you have recently shaved your head/beard or gotten a fairly radical haircut. If you change your hair colour/style/facial hair often, post photos of you with several different looks.

In addition to the face and full-body photos, post a variety of shots showing you doing activities you enjoy (skiing, dancing, dressing up for Halloween, playing a sport, reading a book, skydiving, etc.) for a grand total of three to seven photos.

*Unless you have a child, don't post pictures of you holding children, particularly babies! (People **will** assume they are yours.)*

Don't post pictures of you with girls around your age unless they are clearly captioned, and are preferably relatives (i.e. "My sister and me, Summer 2016).

Don't post pictures of you with your ex, even (especially) if the ex is blurred/cropped out.

Don't post pictures of yourself with multiple girls in the shot unless there is a really good reason for it (i.e. you are an actor and you clearly identify the shot was from a play, you are on a coed sports team, or you are a paramedic, firefighter or police officer, etc.).

Don't post multiple pictures of you in a bar or holding alcohol (one photo shows you like to drink; more than one will make a potential match think all you do is drink).

If you specify in your profile that you don't drink or smoke don't post shots of you drinking or smoking — it instantly destroys your credibility rating.

Unless you have a pet, don't post pictures of yourself with any kind of pet (people with allergies screen these out immediately, and if they don't know will assume it is yours).

Profile pictures are not mugshots or passport photos — SMILE, or at least look like you are thinking about something happy!

For Both Men and Women:

Don't post a photo showing you at your last rather than your current job, particularly if you are wearing some kind of uniform in the shot like construction clothes, scrubs, McDonald's/Tim Horton's uniform, etc. Potential matches will assume that this photo is of you at your current job, and some will choose to pursue or reject the match based on this assumption.

» Usernames

So you have your profile made up and your pictures chosen. Now comes the final piece: the username. Some sites want you to use usernames, while other sites just ask for your first name.

If you are on a site that asks for a username put some thought into it. Prettyboy123, Machoman, CasanovaReborn, HughHefnerthe2nd, Call4aGoodTime2Nite, Mama'sboy, TheStud, HotAccountant and the like are the kinds of names that are likely to turn off many potential matches, or will only attract a very particular kind of person, as are usernames like Snugglebunny, TooCute, Cougargirl, or Hotdate101. Usernames and the opening tagline can be a way to flirt, to show your humour and challenge the opposite sex in a fun, playful way. Don't waste this chance to begin to attract the attention of the kind of person who interests you.

Don't pick a boring username or one that has the potential to be very common such as BlueEyedGal, BlondeHairedGirl, BrownHairedBoy, etc. If someone going through profiles can't remember which one was yours because they just clicked on six with almost identical usernames, odds are they aren't going to bother sifting back through all six in order to contact you.

Don't pick a name that shows low self-esteem or is a turn-off. Loser12, Cheapskate, CreepyGuy85, etc. aren't likely to attract anyone worth dating to your profile. A little self-deprecating humour is fine but literally labeling yourself as a loser or a creep is not a way to present yourself as attractive to others.

If you have moved to a new country run your username by someone who is a native speaker of the language who can alert you as to whether or not your choice of username contains any unfortunate slang.

I once ran across the user name "hussieami." I was a little concerned about it because "hussy" in some places is slang for a woman who is promiscuous and "ami" is French for friend, so that username could be taken the wrong way. When I e-mailed the individual to ask more about how they came up with that name, it turned out that it was actually based on the name of a beloved pet that had passed away.

Not everyone is willing to take the time to clarify the meaning behind a username, so names that contain slang could be costing you potential dates without you even realizing it!

Never use your address, birth date, full name or phone number as your username or part of your username for security reasons.

I read a magazine article once describing a woman who was a dental hygienist whose interest was sparked by a man with the username "toothsleuth." She wondered if he also worked in her field and so pursued the match. Her initial suspicions were correct: he turned out to be a dentist, and if I remember correctly the two of them went on to marry and open a dental clinic together.

Your user name can be used as a tool to both filter potential matches and spark the interest of potential matches, but just beware of double-meanings.

My last username incorporated the words "sword dancer." I chose this name because I had fenced throughout university and, as part of belly dance, had learned to balance a Turkish *kilij* (a type of curved sabre) on my head while dancing. I have always been fascinated by swords and also wanted to convey the fact that dancing was very important to me. This acts as a conversation starter as people ask me about it, although a couple of individuals have been intimidated by it, wondering if references to swords are a dangerous sign in a potential date. While I can see their point I know that the right person for me will find my hobbies interesting rather than intimidating, so for me it serves as a good filter mechanism as well as conversation starter. I later realized that sword dancer could have another meaning for the particularly dirty-minded, but I hoped that by including a picture from one of my dance performances, it would reduce the odds of this interpretation. Now that I am aware this interpretation is possible, I probably won't use this name the next time I post a profile. Much like with the photos, my username and tag line are a matter of trial and error; I keep experimenting until I get the results I'm after.

"Insanity is doing the same thing, over and over again, but expecting different results." *Albert Einstein*

Try to have a good reason for the name you picked as sooner or later someone is going to ask why you chose it. A good reason could be the start of a great conversation, an opportunity to learn more about each other. Something that you decided on "just because" is not likely to come across as interesting for your date, or may indicate that you didn't put much thought or effort into it, turning a potential conversation starter into a conversation killer.

> *"I think usernames are not a bad way to go, as you never know who is looking at your profile. Usernames give you a little bit of privacy. I have three names I commonly use for online purposes such as gaming, and choose one of them to make it easy for me to remember." – Gordon (25)*

» Tone

Avoid using usernames or introductory phrases like "Looking for my prince/white knight/hero" as these can make it sound as though you are looking for a fairy tale rather than a living, breathing human being. Many people don't want to be compared to or compete with a fantasy man or woman. Also be careful of phrases like "Are you man enough for me?" or "I dare you to try to keep up." The undertone in these sorts of statements is arrogant and dismissive. This type of phrase is not a playful challenge; it is just a challenge—and who wants to compete for someone who won't respect them even if they "win"?

» It's Not so Much What You Say – It's How You Say It!

Let's get real—a large majority of North Americans seem to like to watch TV, go to the movies, hang out with friends, occasionally eat out at a nice restaurant, maybe go to a sporting event and/or dancing/to a bar or club once in a while. We are not that different from one another, but at the same time we want our profiles to have some individuality to them.

Don't try to make your life sound like it's something it's not, but do use details to set your profile apart. For instance, rather than saying you like movies, name a couple of your favourite movies, and what you like about them, if space permits.

"I got really sick of seeing profiles that told me what a person would do on their dream vacation, but there were no details as to who they were as a person. Since their profile looked identical to the last ten I had looked at, I had no motivation to contact them/get to know them better." – Gordon (25)

What attracted me to the profile of the girl who eventually became my girlfriend was the T-shirt she was wearing in her profile picture (one with a slightly geeky slogan) and the details of her profile—both conveyed that we might have similar interests/be suited to each other. I could tell that she had also put time and attention into crafting an honest profile, one that would only appeal to certain people instead of everyone and anyone. Since we seemed to have like-minded profiles, I was interested in finding out if we were like-minded in other ways as well." – Gordon (25)

CHAPTER 4

Profiles Are Not Set in Stone

» Be Very Certain of Your Statements

If you put in a phrase like "Seeking a spontaneous girl/guy who is always looking for adventure and is ready to go at a moment's notice," be certain that is really what you want, and be aware of what that statement implies. Someone who can be completely spontaneous is someone with no other commitments—no hobbies, interests or work commitments that need to be worked around. How many adults do you know who have a schedule that is that free? Do you honestly expect your significant other to wait around the house every night and every weekend waiting for your call before they make any plans of their own? Are you looking for a match who is unemployed?

A better statement might be something like "When travelling, I like to plan where I am going and the first night's stay, after that I figure it out as I go. I'm looking for someone who is comfortable with and interested in travelling this way." Or "I don't plan my weekends; each Friday I put up a map of the province/state on a dartboard and then take a day trip to wherever the dart lands." Or "I don't plan my evenings; as soon as I'm off work for the day I look forward to whatever adventure the evening brings. Are you willing to find the adventure with me?" These types of statements imply being adventurous and fairly spontaneous but are specific enough to let potential matches screen you in or out depending on how they like to travel/plan their time. They don't imply that your match can't have any interests or hobbies of their own in their day-to-day life (and it doesn't imply that they can't have a job) but do require someone who can let go of the details and not worry about scheduling every minute of their vacation, evening or weekend.

» Profile Space

You only have limited space to use for your profile, so don't waste it rambling about how you aren't very good at writing profiles, that you never know what to write for these things, that this is your first time trying this, that you can't really convey who you are in set number of words, etc.

» Whoever Is Reading It Doesn't Care!

They don't care that it is your first time writing a profile. They don't care that you are bad at it. They are still going to judge you by your profile because that is all they have to go on. They are trying to use whatever you have written to decide if you are worth any more of their time. They want to know enough about you to say "Yes, I'm curious about learning more about you" or "No, I can't see us working out." To make this choice they need to know a bit about you and about who you are looking for so do your best to describe both. It doesn't matter if it is perfect; just use the space you have for the purpose it was intended!

» Never Be Afraid to Change Your Profile

If, after having your profile up for a couple of weeks/months, you are not getting the attention of the kinds of people you wish to meet, try revising your profile. Most sites allow you to edit it at any time so try playing with your phrasing, changing up details, adding or removing photos or changing which photo you use as your main profile photo.

» Baggage from the Past

Go to a site like PlentyOfFish and spend ten to twenty minutes quickly scanning the profiles. It is amazing how many key phrases in the profiles imply that a person has baggage from his or her past. "Looking for a trustworthy girl who doesn't believe in cheating," "Looking for an honest man who hates lies," Looking for a financially independent man who knows how to treat a girl," "Looking for the last Good Man," "Looking for a man who has a good relationship with his mother," "Mama's boys need not apply," "Looking for a girl who is financially independent and not prone to jealousy," "Not looking to hook up for a night; no, I'm not going to give you money; and no, I'm not going to help you get out of a third-world country."

Most of us hope to find matches that are financially solvent, emotionally stable and have decent career prospects, but putting in phrases like the ones above can actually send the wrong message. Most of them stand out like red flags, warning signs that most financially solvent, emotionally stable people will steer clear of because they don't want this kind of burden in their lives—paying for the sins of your last girlfriend or boyfriend or former husband or wife, or the last Internet-dating con artist you ran into.

Be realistic. Everyone is going to come with some form of baggage, even a total amnesiac (their baggage is that they can't remember what their baggage is). Most people, however, are trying to filter out "radioactive baggage," such as the invisible but raw wounds left by situations such as messy break-ups, people cheating on each other or people taking financial advantage of each other. Much like radioactive waste, even if you don't directly touch it, this type of baggage can still burn you. Since this is the kind of baggage that has the potential to cause them mental, emotional, financial or physical distress in the future, few people want to take the chance that their match's radioactive baggage will spill over onto their lives. Besides, most of us are carrying enough baggage of our own (even of the non-radioactive sort); we have neither the energy nor the desire to take on someone else's!

If you are getting back into the dating game after a bad breakup, a series of bad relationships, or just the end of a long relationship, make certain that enough time has passed that you have been able to put your baggage to bed or, at least, leave it at the door! Some people can get over a relationship in a month, some take sixty days and some take over a year. Don't let society, sitcoms or your friends pressure you into dating anyone if you haven't resolved your issues; no matter how hard you try to hide them they will come out and they will lessen your chances of success with any future date, regardless of whether or not you meet them online. If you are having trouble resolving issues on your own, particularly if they include abuse of any kind, get professional help.

Dating isn't like falling off a horse where it's best to get right back on. Take your time and do what you need to do to be comfortable with who you are and what you have to offer in a relationship. This will pay off by dramatically improving your odds of success in the future.

Keep in mind that no one can "make" you happy, and no rela-tionship can magically "make everything right"—it is your job to figure out how to be happy, what you like and what you don't and how to live a good life. The point of a romantic relationship is to find someone you can be happy with, not someone who can fix you or your life. Someone who already has a happy and interesting life is a lot more attractive as a potential romantic partner than someone who desperately needs someone else to "give" him or her a happy life.

If your profile reads like it was written by a desperate, bitter, unhappy person who requires a "lifeline"—someone to rescue you from the burden of your mess of a life—then you are probably not going to be viewed as an attractive match by anyone worth being matched with! Internet predators such as dating scam con men or women will be drawn like bees to honey, but no one else.

After my last relationship ended I waited a month and a half to start Internet dating again. I had tried everything I could think of to make that relationship work. After it ended, it was quickly apparent that there were some really important lessons about relationships that I had needed to learn, but now that the lessons had been learned it was truly better not to be in that particular relationship. It was clear that relationship simply was not the right relationship for me! This realization let me move on and start looking once again for the right person for me relatively quickly. When this didn't pan out within eight months, I decided to focus on other areas of life. Almost three years later, it is just recently that I've felt ready to start dating again.

> *"I took over a year off after my last relationship. I wanted to make certain that I had put it well and truly behind me before looking to date another girl." – Sam (28)*

» What If You Haven't Had Many, or Any, Past Relationships?

The other side of the relationship baggage coin is displayed by those of us who have had very few or no relationships in the past. There are many reasons why this could be the case (shyness, social awkwardness, body issues, family obligations such as caring for a sick parent or being the breadwinner the family depended on, involvement in highly competitive sports/careers, or just a lack of meeting someone who really sparks your interest) but once a person is in their twenties and beyond, this lack of experience can affect future relationships. Baggage from a lack of romantic relationships in the past can include anger, frustration and/or sadness over the lack.

Once again, look deep inside yourself and be honest about what your issues are. A common issue is self-sabotage of relationships. This occurs when a historical history lack of romantic relationships has left a person with a deep-seated belief that no one can or will love them. (After all, nobody else ever has, so why should anyone be any different?). In this case, the person consciously, or unconsciously, finds a way to self-sabotage or break off the relationship (or even the potential of the relationship) before the other person does.

Someone who hasn't been in a serious relationship is also usually very used to doing everything on their own, and their actions and words may send the message that they don't want or need anyone in their life. Or it can present as the reverse: over-dependence/over-eagerness, where an extremely strong desire for a relationship causes them to jump from just meeting someone to making marriage plans and/or picking out names for their future children.

Get professional help if you need it to resolve or address your feelings, to get out of old patterns of thinking or behaving that are no longer serving you or are holding you back. Similar to those with issues from past relationships, issues from a lack of past relationships will show up if you don't address them before looking for or getting into a relationship. Try to resolve them before you start or be prepared to recognize them and try to mitigate their effects when they do show up. Your chances of finding a successful relationship in the future will be much higher if you do.

For myself, I hadn't dated a lot in my life and it had been a while since I last had a serious boyfriend, so when I first started Internet dating my baggage stemmed from a lack of past romantic relationships. Over the years I had learned to be really independent and this actually created a stumbling block early in my first serious relationship. He noticed that my body language wasn't really conveying interest in him—I didn't try to hold his hand or sit close to him at first. This left him wondering if I was really interested in him at all. A wise friend told him, "Don't ask me; ask her!" We talked about it and we laughed when we realized that I hadn't even been aware I of what I was doing!

I still struggle a bit with this since I am used to being independent and touch isn't one of my primary love languages (Don't get me wrong, I really enjoy it but touch alone just doesn't cut it for me). I honestly appreciate it, however, when a man will hold a door for me, make dinner when I have a hard day at work or take care of me when I'm sick (my primary love language is acts of kindness, so these types of gestures go a long way in helping me feel the romance). I continue to work on my mannerisms so as not to scare guys off by coming across as too independent, but I know that this something with which I still struggle.

» Body Image and Your Profile

The most important thing *not* to do when Internet dating is lie about your physical characteristics. Sooner or later you are going to have to meet the person in person and lying about your body type or your age are the two fastest ways to sabotage any possibility of a relationship. After all, if you are willing to lie about these things, can you really expect the other person to trust anything you say?

Make certain that your profile pictures and your descriptions of yourself match what you look like right now—you don't want to start off the date by having the other person's first thought be, "They don't really look like they did in their pictures!" They say it takes eight positive encounters to undo the effects of one negative first impression and with Internet dating, you are not going to be asked out eight more times if the person doesn't get a good impression of you when you first meet. Don't sabotage yourself.

The Other Side of the Coin – Determining What You Want in a Match

» Look for a Realistic Match

Internet dating is similar to job searches in that we get to list characteristics of our "dream applicant." It's important, however, to remember that Internet Dating is not a magic wand that will reverse all the normal rules of the dating world. In particular, it doesn't erase the rules regarding what is realistic to expect in a likely match. While many people dream of dating movie stars, music/sports celebrities or royalty, most of us accept that this is not likely to happen and so we don't let this fact interfere with our attempts at dating, regardless if we are using the Internet or not.

When Internet dating, very few people set their sights exclusively on celebrities or millionaires but most of us would love to find a modern-day "prince" or "princess" of our very own. "Prince" or "Princess" in this book refers to someone who has the whole package: similar values to our own, a great personality, a great career, a great home, the level of wealth we desire and (to our eyes at least) great looks.

The problem is while almost everyone possesses at least a few admirable qualities or desirable traits, very few people possess *every* admirable quality/desirable trait. Be careful to keep your "wish list" within the possibilities of the human realm rather than romance novels or pop songs. To reject matches because they don't possess every quality on your list is like refusing to hire any candidate whatsoever for a job aside from Sir Patrick Stewart, even when a couple of the candidates have a lot in common with him.

» If a Match Isn't Mr. or Miss Right, and You Don't Want to Waste Your Time...

Never be afraid to indicate interest in the "princes"/"princesses" you come across to see if they return it, but if they do not, don't be surprised or resentful and move on. If you don't, and continually reject other possible matches on the basis that they are not perfect "princes"/"princesses," billionaires or movie stars, then don't blame the dating site or the Internet dating process for your lack of success in finding a match!

Do not set your standards so high that you sabotage any chance of success; you are looking to date a human being who actually exists, and one who is available and honestly wants to date you in return.

» Entitlement

The Entitlement Trap: If you ask for a lot in a mate, make certain you have a lot to offer one. Having a list of 150 must-have traits for the other person when you can't even match 10 of these qualifications yourself is a recipe for failure. After all, if you did find someone with all 150 traits, why would that person want to date you?

It is important to take an honest look at yourself and what you have to offer in a relationship. Ask yourself whether or not what you have to offer is what the kind of person you say you are looking for is looking to find. If you want a man with six-pack abs you might want to ask yourself if you are prepared hit the cross-fit gym, since that is likely where he is to be found. If you want a very skinny and fit girl, prepare to grab some running or ballet shoes, since that is a body type most often found in marathon runners or ballerinas. While these are generalizations, logic indicates that the types of people you are describing as what you want are far more likely to have these interests, habits, lifestyles and beliefs than the ones who don't. This isn't saying that people can't or won't honestly be attracted to different body types or fitness levels than their own; there is certainly more than one stereotypically trim and muscular man who fancies the plus-sized ladies, and more than one skinny woman who is attracted to the plus-sized gents out there. The key is whether you can either share their hobbies or support them in their lifestyle. If you can't, then you may be asking for more than you are willing to give.

It's great to set high standards when you are looking for a mate rather than settling for the first person who expresses interest in you, but beware of the trap of egotistical arrogance. If you reject people on the basis that they aren't bringing enough to the table when you are bringing the same amount or less, do not blame the dating site, or the Internet dating process, for your lack of success in finding a match!

» Beware Biological Limitations when Setting your Standards for a Match

Please remember that despite the frequency with which they show up in the media, certain physiques are almost never found in nature. For instance, finding a woman who is five foot eleven, weighs close to one hundred pounds and still has a C- or D-sized bust is extremely rare since this figure occurs in only a tiny fraction of the world's population. Most women of that height and weight would need breast implants to have more than an A or a small B-sized chest as their bodies simply do not have the body fat content necessary for larger breast development. That degree of thinness may also indicate a thyroid disorder (hyperthyroid) or other metabolic condition, an eating disorder, an exercise addiction or self-esteem issues.

For men, an overly honed physique in which each and every muscle is extremely developed and defined, may indicate an exercise addiction, steroid use, an eating disorder or self-esteem issues.

Try not to set your standards to levels that require unhealthy behaviours or scientific intervention to achieve—this perpetuates artificial and unhealthy stereotypes of beauty and desirability, and it is likely that the unhealthy behaviours will also negatively affect your relationship sooner or later.

» Must-Haves Versus Nice-to-Haves

Here are two hypothetical scenarios to give you a sense of must-haves:

Allison was reading through LIVELOVELAUGH's profile. The photos looked good—he had a really nice smile and he clearly had a similar sense of humour as she did. As she started reading through the profile her hopes began to rise; he sounded like a really great guy. Then she got to the pets section and felt her heart sink. The word that she had been hoping, half praying wouldn't be there was. Spelled out in black and white were the words that ended even the possibility of a relationship for her. Dog. Specifically, "Owns two dogs," and the following words made it clear that the dogs were integral members of his family. Allison's allergy to dogs was so strong that even after going for treatment with an allergy specialist she had to carry an EpiPen with her. Any exposure to dog hair triggered her allergic symptoms, which included her throat starting to close, preventing her from breathing. Allison half cursed under her breath. She couldn't respond to this profile, no matter how much she wanted to.

Nicole read through SunSurfandSand's profile with her usual critical eye. The photo passed and now she needed to look through the details to see if this one was a keeper or not. Ah, there it was. He was only five foot eight and she refused to date anyone who wasn't six feet tall or more. As soon as she read the height SunSurfandSand's profile might as well not have existed since Nicole didn't want to waste her time by reading any further. Click! Nicole was on to the next profile.

Try to keep your list of "must-haves" to five. By "must-haves," I mean things that no matter how good the rest of the profile is, no matter how hot the guy or the girl is in the photo, if these things aren't present you will immediately delete their profile from your list of potential matches. In the above examples, not having dogs is a must-have for Allison while being six feet tall or more is a must-have for Nicole. Common examples of must-haves can include sharing the same religion, sharing the same view on food (vegetarianism) or not having pets (a potential life-or-death must-have for those with severe allergies).

Be cautious when defining your must-haves; stating that your match must have a post-secondary education is fair, as this limits your choices but doesn't exclude all but a small minority of people. Stating that your match must have graduated from Harvard or Yale isn't fair and doesn't help you—all it does is give you an excuse to reject the vast majority of people because they didn't go to a particular school. With this kind of arrogant attitude, Internet dating probably isn't going to work for you, as no one is likely to be "good enough" for you. Your list of must-haves should be personal and reflect what is truly important to you; it shouldn't read like a list of bragging rights about your match that you intend to use to impress your friends.

Allison's choice of a must-have and how she exercises it is great; it reflects her reality and doesn't prevent her from reading a full profile. Based on her response to this profile she could look for similar profiles among individuals who don't own dogs. Nicole's must-have is not so great. It begs the question: If the guy was perfect in every other way but was only five foot eleven—would she really not give him a chance? She'll never know whether SunSurfandSand was right or wrong for her in any other respect because she didn't even bother to read the rest of his profile. In doing so, she prevents herself from learning what attracts her in profiles and what doesn't beyond the question of height. Allison's approach is likely to help her find the right guy for her, while Nicole's is likely to keep her single.

A "nice-to-have" is a trait that in an ideal world you would love for your partner to have but you are willing to compromise on it. One of your nice-to-haves could be for your match to be a graduate from an ivy-league school but your must-have is that they have some form of post-secondary education. This means that you have standards but you are flexible enough to realize you might not get everything you think you want. Try to keep your list of nice-to-haves to below twenty items and if after Internet dating for a while you are finding that you are not having much success, change these up or toss them out. In Nicole's case, if she changed her must-have of six feet or more to a nice-to-have, it would still influence her but it would encourage her to actually read the profiles and double check to see that she is not missing out on great guys who happen to stand an inch or two short of her expectations.

» Having Your Own Biological Children as a Must-Have

For some people having children of their own is a must-have. It is something they want to the point that they will not compromise on it, no matter what they have to do—if they need to they will willingly pay thousands of dollars in fertility treatments, undergo surgery, and get vasectomy reversals. Adoption, or becoming a step or foster parent isn't enough for these people—they want to have their own biological child.

If you are one of these people, make certain that you only respond to profiles that indicate the other partner wants kids. Most dating sites give three to five options to this question: No, Don't Know, Maybe, Someday and Yes/Definitely. If the person puts "No" in their profile, particularly if they have children from a previous relationship, then believe them! "No" means no. Do not respond to these profiles; you aren't going to change people's minds! "Don't Know," especially for guys often translates to "I'd really rather not"—a softer version of no. Once again if having your own children is a must-have for you, these profiles aren't where you should be directing your attention. "Maybe" gives you an opening to ask critical questions: Why did you indicate maybe? What factors or conditions would change that "Maybe" into a "Yes"? (A higher paying job? The right person?) Their answers will tell you important things about how they view having children; if you don't like their answers, walk away.

"Someday," can be good or bad relative to the age of the person in the profile, and the options available on the site. For a twenty-year-old to indicate that they want children someday is pretty reasonable; they are still trying to establish themselves as an adult and get their own life going. "Someday" from a fifty-year-old is another way of saying, "I'd really rather not." Once again, if this is the vibe you are getting then don't hope that you can change their answer, move on to the profiles which have checked off the "Yes, I want kids" box.

When you are trying to decide which answer to check off for this question, be as honest as possible with yourself—if you don't want kids then make certain you make this clear. Do not string people along saying that you might want kids if you honestly have no interest in ever becoming a parent. If you really want kids, indicate this clearly. Having or not having children is a life-altering decision, and regardless of which way your feelings run improve your odds of finding someone you can be happy with by not lying about what you really want. If you lie when answering this question then don't be surprised by your match's shock, dismay and anger when you change your answer later down the road.

Section 2:

So Now You Are Online

CHAPTER 6

The Roadmap

Your profile is up, matches are starting to come in and you are ready to go. Most sites are organized to let you find matches in three ways.

» Way #1: The Searcher

You search profiles and when you find one you like the look of you send a "wink" or a short email, something along the lines of "Hi. I like your profile. I would like to get to know you better. If you would like to get to know me, please respond." Alternatively, on some sites, you click on an "Interested" button. In these cases, the site itself automatically lets the other person know you are interested in them.

» Way #2: The Receiver

You receive an indication that someone is interested in you based on your profile, either through email or the site's alerting function. Now you have a decision to make. You can choose to respond, or you can politely decline interest in the potential match or, if the person who contacted you was way out of line in what he or she wrote, many sites allow you to report abuse.

» Way #3: The Site Matching Function

On sites that have matching functions the site itself will suggest possible matches for you. The number of matches you receive on a daily basis will vary from site to site depending on your settings (distance, age, importance of various values, hobbies, etc.) and on the setting of the site (eHarmony sends you all the matches that fit the parameters of the 27 dimensions of compatibility; Match.com has a Daily Five on the site itself plus a separate selected list of about 10to 20 potential matches it emails to you). If you agree with the site suggestion, then you have to act on it the same way you did in Way #1.

» The First Problem

This is the stage where the lack of rules and commonly accepted etiquette for Internet dating presents its first challenge. In Western/North American culture, it is traditionally expected that the guy will be the one to indicate interest/ask a girl out, and pay for the dates. With Internet dating the rules aren't so clear for both hetero and LTGBQ couples.

I found this point particularly tricky. Some guys still like to take the traditional role of the pursuer and don't like being "hounded," as it puts them out of their comfort zone and creates a role reversal, while other guys appreciate girls taking the initiative to contact them, so I was confused as to which would be the best approach. And let's be honest: it feels very flattering to have someone express interest in you and a desire to get to know you better. While I didn't want to turn potential matches off I did want to be proactive, not just sit around waiting for someone to ask me like a wallflower at a dance. After a long period of trial and error I found what worked for me. When I took on the Searcher role I was most successful, and felt most comfortable, when I limited myself to sending a single wink or a very short email, then waiting for the guy to take the initiative on any future contact. Basically, I thought of it like waving a signal flag that the interest was there, but for a relationship to develop, the guy would have to be the one pursue it. If you meet people in person you can smile and use eye contact to invite them to talk to you, to flirt, or show you might have an interest in them. I mentally compare a wink or a short email as the online equivalent.

Each person who Internet dates should be prepared for some awkwardness at this stage and some trial and error to figure out what works for them. Every person is going to have his or her own beliefs about who should make the initial contact, and is going to have different opinions about each and every contact he or she receive. You may be really interested in someone because they seem perfect for you, but you never hear back from them when you try to establish contact, or they outright decline your interest. Often it is because they have either already found someone else, have stopped checking their profile on the site, or because they don't agree. Be prepared for this.

Limit your attempts to contact another person on the site to one (or if you are really, really interested in the person, two or three). If you don't receive a message back, assume they are not interested and move on. Reasonable people do not play hard to get at this stage of the game. The only exception might be if your computer/Internet connection experiences a glitch or the site freezes or crashes while you try to send the first, second or third email. In this case it really might have been lost in cyberspace and, thus, is worth one last attempt.

Don't get angry when someone declines your interest! There are many reasons for this and rejecting you right off the bat if they don't have any interest in you actually does you a favour—it frees up your time and energy to search for someone who is genuinely interested in you.

I once had a man send me a strong final message after I declined interest in him. This particular gentleman wasn't very good-looking and assumed this was the only reason I had rejected him. He went on a rant about how he might look like a frog but if I gave him a chance would treat me like a princess, and on the general "shallowness" of society. What he didn't check was that while I was in his preferred age range, he wasn't in mine. He was, in fact, more than ten years out of my preferred age range! The reality was he was only slightly younger than my father, something that creeped me out and put him out of my potential dating pool entirely. I'll be honest: his looks played a large part in my rejecting him, but his age was the ultimate deciding factor. Sending me this message (particularly without checking this detail) certainly didn't make me the least bit inclined to change my decision!

Don't harass or insult a person who has declined interest in you! Take the high road and let it go on a classy note—that person wasn't the right person for you.

» The Email Stage

So you have been on the site for a while and congratulations—you have found someone whom you are interested in getting to know who is also interested in getting to know you. You have entered the email stage of Internet dating.

The email stage is an interesting one. In one way it is very important, as it is your first glimpse into what the other person might be like. Here is where the work that you put into your profile and username will pay off—the information contained in them give you places to start a conversation (if your match indicated that he or she likes to travel, you can ask them where they have been, what they liked about the place, etc.). The questions you ask and answers you receive will start to form an impression in your mind and will either make you curious enough to learn even more about the person or will start to indicate that this might not be the great match you thought it was. In another way, however, the email stage is the least important aspect of Internet dating, as it is the least "real" (more about this later).

In your emails, try not to be boring and talk only about generic subjects like sports or the weather unless you are a hard-core sports fan, climatologist, a storm chaser, or the weather had a strong impact on what you did last week. Talk about the things that are important to you: What do you dream of doing with your significant other (dancing under the stars, walking on a beach at sunset, going for a dune buggy ride together, watching game seven of the Stanley Cup, etc.)? Expand upon the traits that are important to you and why. Basically treat email like an expanded version of the profile, an opportunity to elaborate a bit about yourself, what you are looking for and why. The choice you have to make now is do you have enough of an interest in each other to put in the effort to meet face to face? Focus your efforts on trying to answer this question. Pay attention to how you feel about answering the other person's messages. If you dread it or consider it a chore, it's not a good sign. If you look forward to it, and frequently log on to the site to see if the person has messaged you then there might be something there so continue pursuing the relationship.

» How Long Does It Take for Someone to Respond to an Email on the Site?

The answer is it varies. Remember that many people who try Internet dating do so because they don't have a lot of spare time—the obligations of school, their family or their career might interfere with their ability to log on to their dating site accounts.

You may be the kind of person who logs onto a dating site three times a day, every day, while the person you are emailing might only be checking their account once or twice a week. It's really easy to get frustrated with the perceived delay in receiving replies when there is this kind of disparity.

Try not to impose your expectations on the other person or jump to conclusions. Always remember: *You don't have a relationship with another person until you've officially talked about it and agreed to be in a relationship. Until then, all you have is contact with them, not a relationship.*

If the delay in getting responses from your "match" is really getting under your skin, then you might want to ask about their reality and what their expectations are about responding. See if you can either live with their reality (once you know what it is) or if you can work out a compromise. Beware that some people will perceive this behaviour as being "too needy" and may choose to use it as an excuse to reject the match. If this happens, it is unlikely that was the right person for you.

» It's so Frustrating – I Spent Hours Writing an Email Only to Have It Rejected without Ever Being Read!

It is not uncommon to spend time drafting an email and sending it off to someone that you think is a good match and then receiving notification that they have rejected you, even prior to reading the email. You have a couple of choices on how to respond. You can be hurt and offended, or you can be a bit disappointed but relieved, or you can be indifferent. Another person can't "make" you feel anything; how you choose to respond is your choice.

Rejection is painful, but if you don't internalize it as a reflection on you and your "worthiness" then its effects are relatively limited. Remember, you don't have a relationship with this person yet! You also don't know the reality of his or her life, what else is going on with him or her. If a person rejects you, particularly early on in the process, it is actually a favour to you. Either they are genuinely not attracted to you, or they do not have the time to treat you properly, or they have already found someone else they are attracted to and want to pursue a match with. At this stage rejection is usually about them, not you. Is it sad that you took time out of your day to try to attract them with a well-crafted email? A little. Their rejection, however, means that you are free to continue to search for someone who genuinely appreciates the time and effort you put into such an email. Isn't that person the one you would actually prefer to have in your life?

» One Match at a Time? It Depends on the Person

Different people have different preferences regarding how many matches they will try to pursue at any given time. Some people like to concentrate on one at a time and see where it goes, while other people like to be in email contact with two or more and only decide which person to concentrate on after a couple of (in-person) dates. Other people like to play the field and go out with a different person every night of the week.

Unless you have an explicit conversation in which both of you agree that you are only dating each other, and that you are going to take down/hide your profiles, **always assume the other person is activey looking at other profiles and communicating with/seeing other people, either in person or on the site/other dating sites.**

» How Long Does this Stage Last?

Each person will have a different preference for how long they like to spend at the email stage. Some like to email back and forth for months, never meeting in person, while others want to meet in person after only one or two emails. Distance and realistic opportunities to meet will have a great deal of influence on this. Just be careful not to get trapped at this stage; you want a romantic relationship, not a pen pal!

Keep in mind that email is not a real conversation or a real date. It gives you time to think about what you say, find just the right words, look at your answer and edit it before you send it off. Tone is not perfectly conveyed, and there is no body language accompanying it. When you only communicate online it is very easy to imagine what the person is like, and to begin to fall in love with the image in your head. The problem with this is that if the image doesn't live up to the reality when at last you finally meet, you may feel cheated/let down when the other person hasn't done anything!

A fairly common experience is finding that you and your match communicate wonderfully online but when you meet in person, for whatever reason, it is clear that the two of you aren't suited to each other or attracted to each other at all. When at the email stage, always keep this question in the back of your mind, "Do you really want to invest months of time and effort into cultivating a relationship that might end up this way, neglecting other opportunities that come about in the meantime?"

At first I tried emailing for about a month (sometimes even two) before meeting a guy in person (mostly because I had the distance parameters set too wide and opportunities to meet in person were few and far between), but I quickly found this was much too long. I strongly recommend meeting in person after two to five emails, if possible.

"I would e-mail for a maximum of two weeks before trying to arrange a date, to see what the person was like in person." – Gordon (25)

If at all possible, try to meet the other person in person after two to six emails. If you haven't met after two months and you live in the same city/half of a province, this is not a healthy relationship. Do not let yourself be strung along, and do not string anyone else along!

» Moving on from Email

Some people jump right from email to meeting in person, while other couples make use of social networking sites such as Facebook and/or online gaming as a way to get to know each other better. There is nothing wrong with either approach, so don't be upset if the person you are communicating with suggests one or the other. If either meeting in person or communicating only through computers for the first little while is very important to you, then be prepared to explain why to the other person. So long as there is a good reason, most people are willing to accommodate this kind of request. If they are not, do you really want to date them?

» Facebook

If you use Facebook or other social media sites, before you give your online date access to your page, go through your page with a fine-toothed comb. Make certain it is up to date, that you like the profile picture, and the pictures of you and your friends are captioned/easily understood as non-romantic. In particular, make certain to remove any pictures that show you and an ex as a couple! Expect that your date will Facebook "creep" your page, searching through all the different sections to get a better sense of you as a person, so make certain you are comfortable with them seeing what is on it. It doesn't need to have your whole life story, but what is up there should be an actual reflection of who you are today, not who you were two years ago.

Neither person should change their Facebook relationship status from "Single/Looking for boyfriend/girlfriend" to "In a Relationship" unless they have discussed it and both people are comfortable declaring to the world that they are officially each other's boyfriend/girlfriend. If both do agree to this then both people should change it within the same week, preferably on the same day. Normally changing this status only occurs after you have been dating in person, not just though email!

CHAPTER 7

Dating Confidential

» The First Date

So you've finally made it; you have agreed that you want to meet in person. Now comes one of the hardest parts of online dating—moving the relationship from online to real time. Where do you meet? What do you do? Who pays for the date? Do you bring flowers? Do you dress up?

Please be aware that the first date of an online relationship is usually NOT a romantic date! It is a meeting of quasi-strangers where you are trying to confirm whether or not both of you want to get to know the person better. You are also trying to confirm if they are who they seemed to be online. Do not expect to be swept off your feet, or to sweep the other person off theirs. If it is a good match there will be plenty of opportunities for romantic dates, such as date #2. If it is not a good match, even five minutes might seem like an eternity that you will be glad to escape so keep this in mind when planning it.

The following is a list of suggestions and important things to keep in mind, but keep in mind they are just suggestions. Please be true to yourself instead of following a suggestion that doesn't make sense to you.

» For the Men

Even in this era of women's liberation many women are still impressed and flattered when guys take the initiative. Ask women to meet in person—it makes you come across as strong and confident. Offer and expect to pay for the first date—refusing to pay for a five-dollar coffee or a single glass of wine on the first date with someone who may eventually become your wife/husband makes you come off as cheap, not frugal, particularly if you are the one who asked her/him out. Let's face it: single guys are notorious for spending money on things that interest them: video games, MMA tickets, cars, houses, travel, etc. When you don't even offer to pay for a date (particularly a coffee date) most reasonable people take that as an automatic sign that you are not interested in them or in the potential of the relationship and that you are just playing around.

» How Do I Make It Clear I'm Willing/Want to Pay?

Regardless if you are straight or LGTBQ, a good way to indicate you are willing to pay for the date is to simply say something like, "May I buy you a cup of coffee sometime?" or "Can I take you to dinner?" Follow this up at the date by firmly repeating your intention with phrases such as, "I've got this," "My treat," etc.

» Don't Women Feel Offended When the Man Offers to Pay?

The occasional woman will bristle at the offer to pay but most will be flattered by it.

If you feel the expectation to pay for a first date/any date is unfair, please keep in mind the bigger picture. While traditionally women did not pay for the dates, they were also expected to spend money to make themselves attractive to potential partners—they just did it before the date! Even today, the average date outfit and makeup a woman wears costs far more than $5 to $10; in fact, it usually costs as much as or more than the $20 to $75 that her date may spend on her meal on a dinner date and on what he wore to the date! If you feel resentful that you are spending money to attract women, either become a specialist in planning dates that cost nothing, like going for a walk in a public square, or don't bother going on dates.

Paying for the first date doesn't mean you will end up paying for all the dates in a relationship. Usually a couple that lasts more than a couple of dates figures out an arrangement that suits both of them, with the half of the couple that makes more money often paying for the more expensive dates, especially if that person is the one who asked to do that activity. So don't be afraid that paying first sets a dangerous precedent. That being said, nobody, male or female, appreciates a freeloader, and if a date turns into one, don't feel obligated to keep dating that person!

» Remember that Resentfulness isn't Attractive to Anyone!

If you are feeling resentful of your date, please don't repeat whatever is causing the resentment (the type of date, the type of person you are dating, etc.)

Show some initiative and invite the girl to meet in person. If she says she is not ready, wait a week or two, then try again. If she still turns you down, chances of her being the one for you are pretty low.

Be prepared and willing to pay for at least the first three dates (this doesn't necessarily mean you will be paying for them, just be prepared to do so).

Offer to pay for the first date, and if your date declines firmly insist. If she/he still refuses to accept, split the bill.

For Men:

Keep locations public to reassure your date you are not a safety concern.

Remember that with flowers, your date will need to put them in water pretty quickly if they are going to survive, they can't take rough handling, and they represent one more item for your date to juggle (in addition to a purse, coat, etc.). On a first date you may want to bring a single rose rather than a full bouquet to make it easier or just skip the flowers until the second or third date.

Don't go to the movies, a concert, a play, etc. on a first date; you need time and the opportunity to communicate. Three hours sitting silently in a theatre is not going to give you a chance to get to know the other person.

Make it clear that you will meet your date there and that both parties will be responsible for their own transportation (for the first couple of dates, at least, if you met online; for the first date if you have also met in real life).

To keep things interesting for yourself, don't keep going to the same place every time you meet someone for the first time. Go to different restaurants, coffee shops, parks, rock-climbing studios, wine or martini bars, pubs, etc. that interest you. Otherwise, your boredom with the location/activity might affect the date. Use dating as an opportunity to really get to know your city or town.

Avoiding or limiting alcohol to a maximum of two drinks on your first date is a good idea.

Dress up, but dress to suit the location—wear a nice pair of jeans and a well-fitting, clean shirt at the very least! Unless you are going paintballing or to a pottery class, save the loose, wrinkled, ripped and stained clothing for once you get to know each other better. Putting some effort into your appearance shows respect and helps you make the best first impression.

If you don't know what to wear, get a trusted friend to help you pick out an outfit that makes you feel confident.

Plan for the first meeting to last thirty minutes to one hour, but leave room in your schedule for the date to go longer if it is going really well. This is very rare, but it does happen.

Keep your expectations realistic.

Turn your cell phone to mute, and do not answer it or text during the date.

For Women:

Remember that allowing your match to plan and pay for a date DOES NOT obligate you to sleep with him because he paid for the date.

Consider the fact whether or not your date offers to pay for the first date, particularly if he/she proposed it. If he/she is unwilling to invest even $2 to $7 in a cup of coffee for a date that might be the start of a lifelong relationship, you might want to think twice about dating him/her. You can also offer to pay (do "the cheque dance" from *How I Met Your Mother*) but if he/she insists on paying, graciously accept.

Bring enough money to cover your portion (just in case he/she doesn't offer).

Sincerely thank your date for the first date; he/she is giving up time and money to be in your company and even if the date does not work out deserves thanks for this.

Respect the fact that your date is paying for the date by not choosing to order the most expensive item on the menu or a lot of pricy drinks, demanding to go to the fanciest restaurant in town for the first date, etc. In other words, particularly early in the relationship, show a bit of financial restraint, but not to the point of not ordering a dish you really like, in favour of one you don't.

Make certain you are comfortable with the location and transportation. It should be a well-lit public place, and you should be responsible for your own transportation to and from the venue.

Do not have him/her pick you up at your home or workplace until at least a couple of dates have passed.

If at any time you feel unsafe, leave immediately, and bring a fully charged cell phone with you

Avoid or limit alcohol on your first date; two drinks is usually a good max.

Dress up, but dress to suit the location—save your super sexy clothes or your "comfy" clothes for once you get to know each other better.

Most first dates are coffee dates; a nice pair of jeans and a blouse, a casual dress or a skirt and top are usually most appropriate. (A little sexy is good but you shouldn't look as if you are going clubbing if you are going for coffee unless you do happen to be going clubbing after the coffee date).

Even on the second or third date, think carefully about the LBD (little black dress). Since it is considered to be the standby option, it might not help you be memorable. If you do wear an LBD, it should have an interesting cut and truly flatter you. Also, have fun with accessories!

Wear clothing that highlights your most attractive features, not clothing designed just to hide your "flaws."

Double-check what activities you will be doing (and what shoes you will need), so you can dress appropriately (nothing is worse than having to run or hike over uneven ground in high heels).

If you don't know what to wear, get a trusted friend to help you pick out an outfit that makes you smile because you feel confident in it and like the way it looks on you.

Plan for the first meeting to last thirty minutes to one hour, but leave room in your schedule for the date to go longer if it is going really well. This is very rare, but it does happen.

Keep your expectations realistic; a "Cinderella" moment is not likely to occur, so don't let this ruin your date.

Turn your cell phone to mute, and do not answer it or text during the date.

» Alcohol and the First Date

People have very different ideas about how much drinking is too much. Internet dating sites do try to help people avoid extreme mismatches by having people indicate how much they drink: never, occasionally, socially, a couple a week, a couple a day, etc.

For many people a little alcohol, such as one or two drinks, helps them relax, takes off the edge of nervousness and allows them to have an enjoyable evening. For most people, more than four or five drinks pushes them from "socially lubricated" to "socially inept" (and usually pushes their blood alcohol over the legal limit). The more you drink the worse you come across as a date—no matter how well you think you hold your liquor!

It is kind of like alcohol and golf. For many people a couple of drinks help them to relax and perform the fairly awkward action of swinging a club to hit a tiny ball down the fairway. The more an individual drinks, however, the more something that was initially helpful turns detrimental, demonstrated by their increasing number of bad slices or outright misses. On the first date, try to stick to a maximum of two drinks to make certain you give your date the best possible first impression of you. NEVER DRIVE DRUNK!

On a related note, don't keep buying drinks for your date in the "hopes" of getting lucky, or convincing them to keep dating you. This is really obvious and comes across as very creepy to most people, making for a very awkward and uncomfortable date.

One of the weirdest first dates I ever went on was a lunch date at a small Italian café. The first words out of my date's mouth were that he wasn't feeling well but wanted to keep the date, which was very flattering. Concerned for him, and familiar with the café, I pointed out the excellent selection of soups and teas. Over the entire lunch hour, the only thing my date ordered was beer. I have never seen any genuinely sick person order beer, and only beer, nor had I ever been on a lunch date where I ordered food and the other person only ordered a drink. Something wasn't right with this picture—the odds of this guy being an alcoholic seemed way too high, and it was genuinely uncomfortable to eat a meal in front of him when I was the only one eating! (It actually made me feel sympathy for guys who order a steak when their date just orders a tiny salad.) That was the first and last date with that individual!

» Awkwardness

On every first date there is doing to be some awkwardness. We are fighting with two contradictory concepts: being wary of strangers, particularly those we meet online, and establishing the beginning of an intimate relationship. It is no wonder we feel awkward and can have trouble finding the right balance between expressing way too much or way too little!

Some degree of nervousness is almost inevitable and everyone displays nervousness differently. Some people stutter the first time they meet someone, other people say "um" between every three words without even realizing it, and some people display physical reactions like twitching or sweating palms. Try not to jump to conclusions and keep in mind that a certain amount of nervous behaviour is reasonable to expect. Have standards, but try not to judge the other person too harshly; after all, it's likely that you are displaying some nerves of your own!

Finally, a person's behaviour may be influenced by factors outside of his or her control. Allergic reactions to scents or foods may result in unexpected physical or behavioural symptoms, and a diabetic with extremely low blood sugar can resemble someone who is drunk. Once again, try to give a person the benefit of the doubt, but keep this within reason.

On one first date I noticed that the guy was blinking a lot and I wondered if this was a nervous habit or a permanent facial tic. After we had gone on a couple of dates and I noticed he wasn't blinking as much I asked him about it. It turned out that his eyes were very sensitive to light, particularly when it hits at certain angles, and the lighting in the first location just happened to be the worst possible setup for him!

» Too Pushy? Too Uptight? Well, Maybe

It is really easy to get a somewhat false impression of a person on a first date. Without even meaning to, people who are used to being in charge or who are used to doing things a certain way, can come across as pushy. Alternatively, some people may come off as a little too uptight or stiff if they are (very) formally polite the whole time. There is a great scene in the TV series *Firefly* where the doctor explains to the mechanic when she complains of him acting like a "stuffed shirt," that he treats her with extremely formal politeness because that is the way he was raised to treat a lady—the way he was taught to show her respect. If good manners/etiquette was important in a person's upbringing, it is likely that he or she will display an extreme version of this, particularly on a first date. If you find that a date is a "little too" anything" on the first date, give them the benefit of the doubt and go out on a second date. If he or she was *really* pushy, cold, rude, boring, arrogant, boorish, or just plain annoying, call it quits after one.

I laughed when I found out that my first impression at a speed-dating event was of someone who had been to finishing school—since I have never been to one! I grew up camping in tents and helping out with yard work around the house! I was in the debate club in high school and being polite was emphasized in my upbringing, so when I am nervous I revert to formal politeness... but I never realized it was to that degree!

» Mired in Pessimism : The Doldrums Date

In everyone's life, challenges are going to come up. Your parents may be ill, you might have just got passed up for a promotion at work, you might not have had a date in three years, you might have totalled your car last week, or you might be suffering from all of the above at the same time. Regardless of this, be very careful about how you talk about yourself and the challenges of your life when you're on a date, particularly on the first date. If every sentence that comes out of your mouth is negative or pessimistic, the person who is on the date with you is not going to have a good time. They will regard you and your life as a black hole of misery that they need to escape before it is too late. You don't have to be relentlessly cheerful and upbeat but you do have to find a balance between negative and positive comments, or a way to talk about your situation with a little humour. Keep negative comments brief and don't get into a specific breakdown of all the bad things currently happening to you; your date doesn't need every last detail of your life to decide if he or she wants to go on a second date with you.

» Don't Convince Your Date Not to Date You!

If you suffer from low self-esteem you might be able to come up with a hundred reasons someone wouldn't want to date you. Common examples can include the fact that you are older than your date, you have kids, you are not as smart as the other person, you aren't that good-looking, etc. Don't spend your date telling these reasons to the person you're with! Give them a chance to make their own impressions of you and figure out if they like you or not. It is very possible that by supplying your date with all the reasons that you don't believe you are worthy, you could actually talk them out of dating you!

» Completely Flawed or Completely Perfect – Neither Impression Helps You!

Be very careful about self-deprecating humour; if you constantly put yourself down on a date, your date is not going to have a great impression of you. He or she will remember you as you describe yourself! If you don't want to be in your own company, why should anyone else?

Also be careful about how much you talk about your quirks, issues, etc. Pointing out one or two things about you that might be odd or unusual can made you come across as a bit eccentric but interesting. More than this makes you come across as crazy and can turn the date into an awkward therapy session.

On the flip side: don't feel the need to be "perfect." Perfect means you are already complete and have everything you need—there is no space or role for another person in your life.

Try to strike a balance. Make it clear that you want someone in your life but do not need a lifeline.

» Playing the Victim

Bad things may have happened to you in your dating past—people may have betrayed you, abused your trust, stolen from you, etc. Your ex from your last relationship may have set a new standard for drama and horror in terms of bad breakups.

You have every right to feel angry, upset and even scared of going down that road again. You don't have the right, however, to dump all of this on your date, and thereby turn the conversation into a sympathy session to soothe your own wounded ego or a free therapy session.

DO **NOT** regale any future dates with lengthy horror tales from your past, even when they ask about the last relationship you were in, especially on the first two dates! Instead of saying the cheating S.O.B. stole your money and ran off with your best friend," then ranting about how betrayed you felt, take a high-road approach. "My last relationship taught me that I need a man who values honesty and integrity in his relationships." Now your date isn't sucked into your past dating drama, and he or she knows that you have a standard about who you will allow into your life. This is a positive approach that doesn't punish your date for the mistakes made by your ex, and helps to open the door to the potential of a relationship in the future. If you are not ready to take a positive approach, then you might not be in a place where you should be dating yet. Instead, take the time to date yourself—be kind to yourself and figure out who you are and what you need from a relationship in your life.

» The Really, Really, Really "Nice" Guy/Girl

There are times that people describe dates as a "nice" guy or a "nice" girl, but say that there wasn't anything more to them than that. What this usually means is that the other person was so agreeable and easy-going that their presence wasn't actually necessary. Here is an example of trying to plan a date with someone who is this easy-going (and yes, this conversation is almost a word-for-word recitation of a conversation I once had with a prospective date):

Person A: "Where should we go on our next date?"

Person B: "Where do you want to go?"

Person A: "Out for dinner, I guess?
When can we get together?"

Person B: "What day works best for you?"

Person A: "Thursday?" What time should we meet?"

Person B: "Whenever works best for you."

Person A: "Seven p.m. okay?"

In the above example every time a decision needs to be made, the same person is making it. There is no give and take of information, ideas or suggestions. There is no reflection of individual desires, preferences or interests. There is no "getting to know each other" in this kind of conversation.

While a conversation like this is fine once in a while, a relationship in which every conversation is doesn't usually succeed as only one person is contributing anything meaningful to it. In fact, Person A could have this exact conversation without anyone else present, which defeats the point of being in a relationship with Person B in the first place.

Please never mistake the desire to be seen as "nice" as an excuse to be boring. Show your date you are listening to them and respect them, but don't turn into a doormat in the process! If you are not present in the relationship and are contributing nothing to it, then the individual you are interested in has no reason to choose you over any of the billions of other people on the planet!

» Being Nice Doesn't Entitle You to Anything, Particularly Sex!

This may come as a shock but being nice to someone—taking them out for a nice date, buying them dinner, giving them gifts, etc.—doesn't entitle you to anything from them. When you give a gift, you should never expect something in return. There is no unspoken contract between you, no mutually understood obligation in return for your "kindness." The other person isn't obliged to return the "favour" with sex, gifts, or by becoming your girlfriend/boyfriend! If you think that your date owes you anything then you are sorely mistakenly—and a jackass.

Also, if you are nice to someone in the hopes that you will one day be more than friends but give them no indication that you are the least bit romantically attracted to them, do not be shocked, disappointed or upset when you are permanently "friend-zoned." Present yourself as a friend and you will be seen as a friend; present yourself as a potential romantic interest and you gain the possibility of becoming one.

» One Date Does Not a Match in Heaven Make

No matter how well a first date went, do not assume that the two of you are meant to be. Let the other person know that you really enjoyed the date and you would like to go out again, or invite him or her to go on the next date but don't be surprised or devastated if he or she turns you down.

DO NOT TRACK DOWN (through the phonebook, Facebook, Google, etc.), STALK OR OTHERWISE HARASS A PERSON if he or she chooses not to go on any more dates with you (i.e. by showing up unexpectedly at his or her home or workplace). Crossing this line puts you clearly into the creepy category of Internet daters!

It is a person's right not to feel the same way that you do! Just because someone goes out on a date, or even a couple of dates, with you does not mean you have a relationship. Having a conversation where you both indicate you choose to be in a relationship puts you in a relationship. Nothing else! This is particularly true for an exclusive relationship!

Personally, I find someone jumping from one pleasant meeting/date to thinking that we have an instant exclusive dating relationship just as unappealing as someone automatically expecting to sleep with me on a first date. How about you?

> *"Can you become best friends with someone*
> *you just met, just by asking their name?"*
> *– Ichigo Kurosaki's Inner Hollow, Bleach, Episode 39*

» **Judge the Potential of Relationships by Actions, not Assumptions**

A great book to read in advance of starting to Internet date is *He's Just Not That Into You by Greg Behrendt and Liz Yuccillo*. The main message is *do not* start making up assumptions or excuses for your date as to why he or she never called you back (he or she must be in the hospital/have lost all your contact information/have been intimidated by you/have not been over their last relationship, etc.) The simplest and most likely answer to what happened is that your date did not return your feelings and moved on to the next possible match.

Judge people by their actions, not your assumptions as to why they are acting the way they are. Focus on choosing what action you will take in response to their actions. For example, if a person fails to contact you after a date, you can choose to send them one invitation to go on another date or you can choose to forget about them. Set standards for yourself, such as if they don't respond within two weeks then you will delete them from your list of potential matches and move on. Such standards empower you by defining to the world how you expect to be treated and what sort of treatment you simply don't have the time for.

A common story among Internet daters, particularly women, is that of being asked rude, vulgar and inappropriate questions either at the email stage or on first dates. This is treatment no one has the time for. Delete these matches, report them to the site, and do not give them the benefit of the doubt or multiple chances to hurt you. You owe nothing to anyone, and you are not in a relationship or obligated to behave in ways that make you uncomfortable or to put up with behaviour that is disrespectful.

CHAPTER 8

Dating Dilemmas

» I Got Stood Up! On the First Date!

This has thankfully been really rare in my experience but it is not fun when it does happen.

I had been emailing back and forth with one individual and he had impressed me by taking the time to write more than most guys do in his emails (at least in my experience). He seemed genuinely interested in meeting me and we made arrangements to meet at a coffee house on a Sunday night. He was getting back from a business trip that day and I had a couple of performances in a dance festival earlier that afternoon. When planning the date, I was a little uncertain about planning to meet right after his travels (since I'm not at my best after getting off the plane from a long flight) but he insisted it would be fine. The dance festival ended up finishing a bit late so I didn't have time to fully remove the stage makeup or fix my hair and still make it to the date on time. Punctuality is important to me so I settled for quickly changing my clothes and hurrying to the arranged place. Ironically, I got there early as I found parking more easily than I expected. After looking around to see if he was there yet (he wasn't), I sat down and waited. And waited. And waited...

It is an awful feeling to be sitting there waiting for someone whom you've met online but don't really know yet. It's difficult to decide whether to give the person the benefit of the doubt or just be angry that the date you anticipated evaporated into thin air.

In my situation, rather than waiting all night I made a pragmatic choice: after waiting twenty minutes I would order myself a large hot drink and then stay long enough to finish it. If he didn't show up by then I was out of there. He never did show, so after 40 minutes, once I finished my drink, I went home. Because of the positive impression from the emails and the fact that he had indicated he was travelling, there was a slim chance that a reasonable explanation such as a flight delay was behind the no-show, so I sent him an email asking for an explanation. After two days he still hadn't contacted me. That's where I drew the line. I am a reasonable person and will make exceptions for unavoidable circumstances. But I am not willing to put up with people treating me poorly or inconsiderately, particularly those I date. This one, despite his good first impression, clearly wasn't the right person for me.

If you get stood up, set parameters for yourself in terms of how you will react. Based on what you know of the person so far, how long are you willing to wait for them to show? Did you give them your cell phone number, and if so, have they tried to call? Use increments like fifteen or twenty minutes ("If he/she is not here in twenty minutes I'm out of here"). Once this limit passes, unless the person calls you and lets you know what is causing the delay, leave. You are not responsible for him or her, and odds are the person has not been in a horrible accident, lost your number, etc.

Create standards for yourself and stick to them—this shows you respect and value yourself and aren't willing to put up with those who won't honour your standards. The right match for you will respect you, and will show up to the date or will provide you with a reasonable explanation and apology in a timely manner.

» First Date Tales

"The very first Internet date I went on was terrible. She wasn't comfortable meeting me alone so it ended up being kind of a double date with some friends of hers who were a couple. Not only did I get a very different impression from her in person compared to her profile, the other couple made things even more awkward by discussing subjects I considered inappropriate, such as their sex life. As this was the first time I had met them I really didn't want to know that much about them! Thankfully, each of the first dates I had with other matches I met on line were exponentially better, culminating with the one where I met my current fiancé
– Gordon (25)

» What if You Never Get Asked Out For a Second Date?

If you are finding that you get asked out on a lot of first dates and never asked out on second, then the sad truth is that you may be the problem. You may be displaying behaviours or giving off vibes you are not aware of but that are eroding your dates' interest in ever seeing you again.

» Use the Resources that Are Available to You

There is a great book Rachel Greenwald called *Why He Didn't Call You Back*. In it the author applies the exit interview technique developed for when people leave their jobs to work elsewhere to dating. For ten years, she researched why guys would go out on one date with a woman then never call her back, gathering a very interesting assortment of answers from a thousand real people. While it is mostly written about why men wouldn't call women back, there is a short chapter in the back about why women wouldn't call men back for a second date.

If you seem to have a lot of trouble moving past the first date, try reading the appropriate sections to see if your lack of success with first dates is due to your approach or the impression you are giving your date. Some of the most common reasons in the book include giving the impression that you would be a great boss rather than a great date, coming off as too boring, or too interested in your own agenda. Others include being too focused on your date's income, showing too much bitterness towards your ex, or hyping yourself up so much prior to the date that meeting you in person is a letdown for your date! (You sold them on meeting Superman and showed up as Clark Kent).

Throughout the book the author makes a great point—that the purpose of a first date is not to begin to establish a lifelong relationship, but to get to date two. You shouldn't try to be something you are not, but you can modify or soften your approach a little on the first date so that you give the opportunity for a relationship half a chance.

» Initial Attraction - Fireworks Versus Campfires

Fireworks and campfires both light up the night with heat and light but are very different in terms of impact and endurance. Fireworks are spectacular flashes of light that quickly fade away, leaving you longing for the next, while campfires give off a steady light for hours, drawing you into their circle of warmth. Love and attraction can work the same way. There are some people who fall in love with the flash of initial attraction that usually occurs on the first date or two. This works for a time, but much like a firework this type of love often fades, particularly as aging, having children, health issues, etc. changes the physical characteristics of our bodies. In good relationships the couple then moves to the next stage—the campfire type of love. Campfires aren't as flashy and might take longer to get going, but they can burn all night long—so long as you keep adding fuel to the fire. Other people skip the flashy fireworks stage and jump right to the campfire version of love, and there is nothing wrong with this!

Based on my dating experience so far, I have come to realize I am probably more of a campfire type of person than a fireworks type of person in my love life. I enjoy the beauty of fireworks and admire them from afar, but I have never fallen in or out of love easily, and surface physical attraction or intellectual compatibility alone isn't enough for me. This presents a challenge when Internet dating as the first part of dating is mostly about the flash of fireworks—the instant attraction/chemistry. It can be frustrating and disappointing when a part of you hopes to experience it but it simply isn't there. At first I was giving myself a really hard time about this and feeling disappointed and frustrated, but I have realized that it is important for me not to beat myself up about this—it is simply who I am.

Every once in a while when I get frustrated with the first-date process, I need to remind myself that with my personality the campfire type of love is what I am actually trying to find and that this type of love often can't be easily found in the first couple of dates.

A campfire type of love is only obvious when you let someone close enough to you to see you vulnerable and help you when you need it—the same way that the true value of a campfire isn't recognized until the night grows dark and cold (or you have marshmallows, chocolate bars and graham crackers on hand).

There are some dates that are clearly going nowhere after the first date and it is okay to walk away from those ones without regret. I have, however, learned that for me if the first date is at least okay and there is a bit of an ember beginning to glow, then I owe it to myself and my date to go on at least two or three more dates. I need to see if that ember fizzles into friendship (the usual result), or if it starts to build into a romantic fire. If after two to three dates, I start to feel the beginnings of a romantic fire, then I need to think very strongly about simply dating the guy for a couple of months and if it isn't working out by then, simply walking away at that point. To find the type of love I want, I need to give a guy the opportunity to demonstrate if he can be the campfire I need to keep warm for the rest of my life.

» Stage of Life Differences

A common problem, which often puts the brakes on new relationships, can rear its head on the first date or later in the dating relationship. This problem is stage of life differences.

One way this presents itself it when one person is still is school while the other is holding down a job. Generally speaking, school is a selfish time—people invest a lot of time and energy in their education in order to have a better life down the road. During this time, they require a lot of support and patience from the people around them. This support can take many forms. Sometimes it is financial or it can also be expressed in the form of understanding and consciously choosing to put off things such as getting married or starting to have children until a later point in time. When both halves of a couple are in school, it is easier for them to support each other as both are at the same stage of life. When one half of a couple has completed his or her education, it can be much harder.

I have experienced this twice in my dating life. The first serious relationship I had while Internet dating was with someone who was finishing his law degree, while I had already been part of the workforce for a few years. We had been dating for just about two years and, to me, a relationship is either going somewhere after two years or it isn't working. After graduating and successfully passing the bar, he felt that he had spent his whole life in school and wanted to "experience life" before settling down. Even after talking it out, he wasn't willing to compromise on this point, and he wasn't willing to try "experiencing life" with me as a couple. Our stages of life were not compatible with each other.

My second experience was more recent. I went on a date with a very nice guy around my own age. He had also been in the workforce for several years, in construction. In this case, my date realized that his current field of work wasn't where he wanted to be for the rest of his life. Oddly enough, he too had determined that he wanted to go into law and was currently looking into universities to start his undergrad degree. It was going to take more than eight years for him to finish his schooling as he was planning to attend school part-time and work part-time. He was not looking to "settle down" into a serious relationship or for at least six to seven more years, which was problematic for me. Once again I was faced with the prospect of getting into a relationship with someone who was planning to devote his life to a different stage of life than I am at. There was nothing wrong with him or with me, but since we were in different stages of life, I decided that we were probably not the best match for each other and chose to stop dating him.

» Biological Clocks and the Instant Family

While the "ticking biological clock" is a commonly joked about female condition, it is more and more common for some men to also display a desire for an "instant family." It seems that most men spend about a decade (give or take a few years) after they finish their schooling to establish themselves in the world (find a good job, move up in the company, buy a house, buy a car, reap the benefits of the bachelor lifestyle). Then, somewhere between the ages of thirty and forty, many suddenly reach the "settle down" phase where they want to get married and start a family. What is distinctive about these men is that they don't want to take their time and let a relationship grow at its own pace; they want to find someone and get married ASAP and start having children so they can get on with their plan for the rest of their life. Having a wife and a family seems to be more of a mark of success to these men or another item to check off of a five-year plan than it is about finding the right person.

Just as a lot of guys are made very uncomfortable with being seen as sperm donors when all they want to be at that moment is a casual date/boyfriend, women can also be made very uncomfortable by men with this expectation to abruptly change their entire lifestyle from single, independent woman to wife and mom or walking womb (a.k.a. "baby momma") in one fell swoop. This is particularly true for women who are very successful in their careers and who genuinely enjoy them, especially if on the first couple of dates they get the vibe that the man is evaluating them more as a potential mother to his future children than a girlfriend or wife.

If you are a woman who desperately wants to start having children right away or a man who is desperately looking for someone who wants to get married and start a family with you right away then recognize that this desperation is likely to turn off many of your potential matches, unless they also share this desire.

» The Problem of Desperation

Desperation comes through loud and clear and most people are not attracted to it—the usual response is to try and get as far away from a desperate person as possible. If you are unsuccessful after several months of dating, then honestly evaluate how much your desire for the next stage of life is interfering with your current stage.

Try relaxing and seeing where the relationship goes on its own — give it time to grow. If you are pushing to drive a relationship from meeting someone for the first time, to officially dating them within days, to moving in with them within weeks, and then pushing for marriage within months, know that you are going to come off as desperate. Most people will be turned off by this behaviour.

» Not Ready to Settle?

The flip side of the "Settle NOW!" phenomenon is the "Eternal Bachelor/Bachelorette" syndrome and the "Fear of Commitment" phenomenon.

"Eternal Bachelor/ Bachelorette" types are men and women in their late twenties to late forties (and sometimes into their early fifties) who still want the freedom of being twenty-one with parental financial backing/ a sugar daddy or momma. These individuals are content to let a woman or man take care of them but they want to travel and spend their days playing and moving from city to city or travelling from one country to the next to experience the world; they have no interest in settling down. If you are still in this stage of life, no matter what your age is, do the women and men of the world a favour and make it explicitly clear in your dating profile that you are not looking to settle down in the near future. This is especially important if you are a heterosexual man. Due to biology, women don't have as much time to play around as men if they are interested in having kids. Don't interfere with their search for someone who actually does wants to settle down; if you date a person for two or more years with no intention of settling down and getting married, that is two or more years they have essentially wasted on you. Live your life the way you want to but don't interfere with the way that other people want to live their lives by leading them on.

Give yourself a specific time limit—such as one to two years—to date a person (particularly if marriage and kids are an important part of what you want in life). If the other person is not moving towards something more serious, like getting engaged, by the end of that time period, move on. Don't waste your time on someone who is stuck at a more juvenile stage of life than the one you are at.

Don't "take care" of an adult the way a parent looks after a child—this is not your role as a girlfriend/boyfriend and will likely kill the attraction between you or lead to resentment over time. Do yourself a favour and think very hard about staying in a relationship with a person who wants you to play "parent." Someone who is serious about you and serious about your future together will work towards building something with you. A person who isn't serious will simply mooch off you for as long as he or she is able.

Fear of commitment can show up in either sex. Think of Robin from the early seasons of *How I Met Your Mother*. Here was someone who was terrified of being trapped in a relationship and unable to live the life she really wanted. Rather than enjoying each date for what it is, this type of individual tends to sabotage relationships as soon as they show any signs of becoming serious. Dating someone with commitment issues can be very tough as it is baggage that individual is bringing to the relationship and the other person shouldn't have to deal with it.

"And I know she's afraid to commit but it's only our second date." —The Offspring, "She's Got Issues"

CHAPTER 9

Romance, the Friend Vibe and Getting Lucky

» Make an Impression with Your Second Date – Let the Romance Begin!

Date number two is your opportunity to make a lasting impression. You have already met each other and know that you are interested enough to spend at least a little more time in each other's company, so date number two is already off to a great start. The objective of this date is to have fun together, and to begin building a relationship. The exact nature of the date will depend on each couple's interests, but it should be based on doing something both people enjoy. There is research to suggest that doing an activity that gets the heart beating quickly (like dancing or rock climbing) can be good for developing relationships, as the other person will attribute their "quickening heartbeat" to the person rather than just the activity, but this also depends on the couple. If either of you is afraid of heights or is not in the best physical shape, for instance, rock climbing might not be the best choice!

» Tales of Second Dates

It had been a couple of weeks since our first date, so I wasn't sure if this particular guy was interested in me despite how well the first date had gone. Then he phoned me up one evening and said that he had bought some symphony tickets from a buddy who wasn't able to use them and asked if I was interested in going. In my previous Internet dating experience no one had ever jumped from a "coffee date" to something like the symphony, so the grandness of the gesture helped to quell any doubts about whether or not he was interested. We met at the theatre, and I liked the fact that when he realized he was going to be about ten minutes late he took the time to phone me and let me know. This reinforced the good impression I had of him from our first date, and helped our second date get off to a good start.

Another second date that I enjoyed was going to dinner and a corn maze. The day of the planed date, my match checked ahead and discovered that the restaurant we were originally planning to go to closed an hour before we planned to meet. We changed to a different restaurant and had a nice supper, which he kindly paid for. We then went to a corn maze that was set up as a quiz—it had a number of stations with multiple choice questions at each directing you to go right or left. The first set of questions was based on children's nursery rhymes and songs. It was fun seeing what we could remember and finding out that we both were willing to be silly. In the second half of the maze, the questions were based on animal trivia and both of us learned a couple of interesting facts. This stage of the maze was more difficult, and we answered one of the questions wrong so it took a lot more time to work through this stage. It was good to see what we both acted like when things weren't going smoothly. The time it took to go through the maze gave us a lot of time to talk.

I would have never gone on the maze for a first date, and I'll admit I was a little wary of it even for the second date, since my match and I were still essentially strangers. If the maze didn't have a manned booth and staff that would find you if you called for help (i.e. truly got lost), I probably wouldn't have felt comfortable going into the maze; in fact, I might not have gone in at all.

While it is important not to be too cautious, it's also important to look out for yourself when meeting new people. Never put yourself into dangerous circumstances with someone you don't know.

Another second date that I enjoyed involved going to "A Taste of" festival where booths from many of the city's restaurants were set up so you could sample their cuisine. It was fun to walk around talking while we tried different dishes. This gave me a good feeling for my date as a person and let me get a glimpse into many different aspects of his personality.

» Lessons from Second Dates

I am a complex individual, and while I am comfortable with camping and hiking, I also have a side that likes going to the symphony and the opera, and as a child I dreamed about dancing at a New Year's gala or going to a masquerade ball. I love dressing up and, to me, taking the time and effort to dress up for an occasion enhances the experience and is a way to get out of the rut of day-to-day life. I need to find someone who not only accepts this part of me but who will go to the trouble of dressing up for a romantic date and who enjoys the experience of this kind of evening. To me, a date is special and worth taking the time to dress up for, and helps to distinguish it from just going out with friends.

While Internet dating, I have noticed that the first couple of dates tend to be very casual. The first date is often a coffee date and the second date is often activity-based or dinner at a casual restaurant. In the city where I live there are lots of festivals in the summer so it is common to be invited to go to one festival or another for the second date, and these are casual events where dressing up equals a simple sundress or a nice shirt and jeans. While these dates can be a lot of fun, they don't give me any idea if a guy is interested in/willing to put some effort into a fancy night out. I have often been a bit startled when my date comments that I look "fancy" or "really dressed up" when I am wearing jeans and a nice but casual shirt on the second date and some nice jewellery, as this is far from my own definition of "dressed up."

I have learned that if I don't get the chance to go on a more formal date on the first couple of dates, then it is a good idea for me to try to create that opportunity on the third or fourth date. By asking to go to a really nice "romantic" restaurant or a fancier event I get to see if my date is willing to put in the effort to go such a place and to dress up a bit himself. He doesn't need to don a James Bond-style tuxedo (although that would definitely get bonus points), but a guy who takes the effort to put on something fancier than jeans shows me that we are compatible in this way. My married female friends tell me that a guy never puts as much effort into impressing you as in the beginning stage of the relationship, so if he won't put forth the effort while dating I can't expect him to start doing so once we're married. I'm not interested in guys who won't put it in the effort to impress me as a date.

» The Friend Vibe

When you meet someone new online the first thing you hope for is romance—that this will be the guy or girl who will be your romantic partner for the rest of your life. Most often this doesn't happen, and often all you get is the friend vibe. This is when you enjoy each other's company, but there is no physical attraction or chemistry between you. You have no urge to hug or kiss your date at the end of the night. Or, if you do, you feel nothing, or it feels wrong. You can't picture yourself in bed with the person at any point. You don't especially look forward to his or her calls or emails. There is no sense of anticipation about the next time you will meet. You might be able to picture yourself going to the movies with this person, watching sports together or doing another activity that you have in common, but in terms of intimacy there is just nothing there, nor is there the hope that anything more could develop.

There is nothing wrong with this! You are looking for the right romantic partner for you, but this does not mean that you can't meet good friends along the way. In fact, it would be fairly odd if you didn't meet people with similar interests to you with whom you could be friends with, if not necessarily lovers, since your profile draws the interest of people who are similar to you.

If after going on a couple of dates all you feel for your match is the friendship vibe, the most important thing is to be honest and let the other person know. Let him or her know that you want to be friends and then see how he or she reacts.

If the other person feels more chemistry for you than you do on your end, he or she probably won't want to be friends as this leaves them in an awkward position. If they want to concentrate their time and effort on finding romantic matches rather than making or developing new friendships, then they most likely won't want to be friends. That is fine; don't get depressed or upset. Once in a while you will meet someone who honestly returns your feelings and will work on developing a good friendship with you.

You need to let a potential match know how you feel so they can decide for themselves how to proceed. It takes time, energy, effort and money to date. If you are taking up someone's time by leading them on when you don't have a romantic interest in them then you are being selfish. Respect them enough to say "Sorry, I don't think you're the one for me, but I think we could be friends."

» Heating Up the Sheets: Sex and the Third Date

Drop your expectations about sex on the third date. Every couple will be different in determining when the right time to start having sex is (some couples will have it within the first two dates while others wait until they get married). There are a lot of excellent biological reasons beyond avoiding getting pregnant and STDs not to jump into having sex too quickly (such as the fact that the body's release of a variety of chemicals during sex, such as oxytocin, can create a bond before you are even sure you want one, and the likelihood of women having a satisfying sexual encounter before they get to know a man can be pretty low), but the definition of "too quickly" will depend entirely on the individual.

The fact that you start as total and complete strangers prior to meeting online often means it may take a little longer to be comfortable with the idea of being intimate with the other person, so the old "third date" rule might correspond to the sixth, ninth or twelfth date. Be aware, however, that thanks to the influence of the media constantly projecting first-, second- or third-date sex as "normal," each person in the couple could have a different definition of what "taking things slow" or "waiting to have sex" means.

If you really want to simply hook up for a one night stand, that's fine! So long as you are very clear that's what you are looking for. This lets potential partners who are looking for the same thing find you and no one gets hurt. Don't lead anyone on by saying that you are looking for a relationship if you are not interested in more than a hook-up; it's cruel and a waste of both of your time.

Please be careful to be honest about your motivations for agreeing to sleep with someone. Despite how some people (usually women) are often socialized, remember that you don't owe anyone sex for any reason, and it is okay for your date to be disappointed if they don't get it.

DO NOT BE PRESSURED INTO HAVING SEX if you don't want to/don't feel ready yet. If he or she is the right person for you, he/she will wait until you are ready.

Keep in mind that sleeping with someone isn't a way to "make them" want to date you as a girlfriend or boyfriend, so do not consent to or initiate sex on the premise of "getting" that status.

Women, it is important to be aware that some men specifically go online to find one-night stands. To "hook-up with an Internet dirty" is one term I have heard men use to describe this. While not all guys seeking sex are this slimy, please keep in mind for many men the decision about sleeping with a woman is not connected to whether or not he wants to have a relationship with her. In other words, don't sleep with a man thinking that doing so will "make" him yours or "create" a relationship.

Many dating experts advocate some version of the *Millionaire Matchmaker*'s phrase, "No sex without monogamy" in order to find real love. The right to touch you and the right to have sex with you is a privilege, particularly the exclusive right to do so. If you don't have standards around how to earn this privilege and you just give it away because the man/woman you are dating wants to/ thinks you owe them this, then you are failing to recognize your own value. You have every right to demand to be in an official—and particularly in an exclusive—relationship prior to having sex as part of your standards, if that is important to you.

If you are having sex, please remember to practice safe sex! Both people should be responsible for this, doubling up on contraceptive methods (condom and the pill, condom and IUD, etc.), if possible, and having a spare condom or two handy. So women, do not be afraid to throw one in your purse or put some in your nightstand just in case!

A man or woman who refuses to practice safe sex is a giant red flag: if you sleep with them it is literally as if you are sleeping with everyone they have ever slept with. Beyond the life-altering reality of pregnancy, sexually transmitted infections and diseases are a very real possibility. The longer someone plays this game, the more it becomes a question of when they will get an STI/STD or someone pregnant rather than "if." Protect yourself and think very hard about continuing a relationship with someone who is willing to take this sort of risk.

» One Last Comment on the Subject of Sex

Being too prepared for sex very early in a relationship, or expecting your date to be completely prepared earlier in the dating relationship than they are comfortable with can be a turn-off. Keeping an overnight bag stashed in your trunk at all times in case you get lucky can send the message that you are a player who just wants to get laid and that you are not necessarily looking for a long-term relationship. A woman or man who expresses surprise that their date doesn't have such a kit handy at all times can also come across poorly, especially early in the relationship. It begs the question of what kind of relationships you are used to having. Quality men or women don't want to feel as if you are dating them just to be able to get another notch on your bedpost. This isn't about people's value going down if they have a lot of sex. People's value is intrinsic and can't go up or down no matter how many, or how few, sexual partners they have had. The turn-off I'm talking about is giving a date the impression that he or she is just being used for sex.

» Time's Up: What's Your Answer? Date #5

In Internet dating, date five is often the make-or-break date. In other words, this is the point at which you decide if a match is worth pursuing and you move from online dating to just dating. This can be as casual or as formal a dating relationship as you both want, but this transition is marked by both individuals agreeing to be in a relationship.

If you don't have this talk, then do not assume you are anyone's boyfriend or girlfriend! Do not assume that you are in a relationship! Do not assume that that the person isn't seeing anyone else—he or she could be dating a couple of other people or still checking profiles online. If you decide not to date the person, date five is usually the one by which you decide that this match just isn't right for you.

The fifth date is usually when this happens because if you were still a little uncertain by the third date, you probably needed a couple more opportunities to get to know each other better or to see things went. Most people seem to feel that by going out on five dates with someone in addition to emailing and texting between the dates, they have given the relation-ship a fair chance. If things still aren't as you hoped after this much time has passed, then there is likely little hope for the relationship.

While most people are not looking for a grand declaration of everlasting passion or eternal commitment by date number five, many are looking for some sort of sign that you are interested in them and in being in a real relationship with them, or at the very least getting off the Internet dating site. Even if you are not quite at the level of "going steady" or being exclusive, it is worth talking about how you feel about each other and what you see happening next.

Most reasonable people are willing to slow things down and continue going on dates if you express interest but explain you are not quite ready to commit to an exclusive relationship. If they are not even sure you are interested, however, very few will want to continue going out with you when they could go back online and find someone who is genuinely interested in them.

There are certain physical signs that on the third date convey mixed messages, but if they are still happening by the fifth date, likely spell doom for the match. These include "the peck," and "the personal space divide." "The peck" is a closed-mouth kiss, akin to the ones seen in movies featuring Europeans greeting each other or saying goodbye, where they give each other a short peck on each cheek, or sometimes on the lips. It is also akin to the kisses that mothers sometimes give their children on the forehead before they send them off to school. In Internet dating it is not uncommon for a couple's first kiss to be a peck on the cheek or lips. This is particularly true if one person has had a lack of romantic relationships in their past (and so is very awkward about moving into an intimate relationship) or if one person is still not quite over their last romantic relationship. Their mind might be ready to move on but their body could still be struggling with more intimate forms of kissing. It could be as simple as they want to kiss you but they have a cold sore developing and don't want to risk passing it to you. If your partner's reactions towards kissing are confusing to you, you need to bring this up to find out what his or her reasons are for holding back in this area.

"The Personal Space Divide" includes such things as refusing to hold hands, avoiding sitting next to each other, awkwardly embracing, flinching/being startled by unexpected touches, keeping arms crossed protectively across one's body, never looking each other in the eye, etc. Not everyone is comfortable with public displays of affection but when these behaviours are happening even in private is when most people start thinking there is something wrong. You may or may not be aware that you are displaying these behaviours, but they signal disinterest to your match with a capital *D*. Most people are considerate of not coming across too strong at the beginning of a relationship when you are essentially strangers to each other, but as each date progresses, if these behaviours don't diminish, you can begin to feel as if the other person is not interested in you, which will usually lead to you giving up on the match by date three and most certainly by date five.

Section 3

Beyond Internet Dating

CHAPTER 10

Reality Re-Entry

» The Friend Test

So you have been on a couple of dates, and you and your match seem to be hitting it off pretty well. Now is the time that you will most likely be subjected to the "Friend Test."

The Friend Test takes place the first time you meet one or more of his/her friends. Usually your match will carefully choose who he or she wants to introduce you to first—it will be someone he or she trusts to provide honest feedback. With Internet dating, many of us want reassurance from someone whose opinion we respect that they also get a good impression from the person we are dating. The occasion also serves as the test case; if it goes well, you will likely be introduced to more friends and possibly colleagues and/or family. If it doesn't go well, then your match will have some difficult decisions to make.

Most friends who participate in the Friend Test are looking for a couple of things:

1) Do you come across as genuine and/or genuinely interested in their friend?

2) How do you treat people who are important to your match, particularly when your match is out of sight/earshot? We have all heard stories of people who seem really nice when their boyfriend/girlfriend is beside them but when the boyfriend/girlfriend leaves the room, a different side to them comes out. The friend is there to look after their friend's interests, to give the kind of critical feedback that someone swept up in passion might not be able to process or have the opportunity to see.

Friends are also there to gauge how you will fit in with their social group. Could they picture you at New Year's, Grey Cup or Super bowl parties with the gang? Could they see you fitting in on a camping trip or a group vacation? The hope is that you will fit in well enough that the idea of including you in future social activities isn't totally repugnant. Because, let's face it, when your best friend(s) and your boyfriend/girlfriend don't get along, it inevitably leads to tension and can even lead to the eventual destruction of the friendship(s) over time.

When you meet your match's friends, don't try to be someone you are not, but also remember that if these are the first people he/she has chosen to introduce you to they are important to him/ her so try to get along with them. Think carefully about the kind of jokes you tell, or the comments you make, particularly right at the beginning before you get a chance to see how your match and his or her friends interact, what kinds of things they say to each other, how they talk about other people, etc.

A good match will warn you about any sensitivity that you need to know about (i.e. their best friend's bad first marriage, strong religious convictions, strong political views, fanatical views on sports teams, etc.) BEFORE you meet his or her friends, but it still helps to be a little cautious in case he/she forgot to mention something.

Be aware that you might need to be willing to join in an activity that's not in your wheelhouse (i.e. go to a baseball game or play a game of laser tag) if that is what your match and his friends like to do. By showing an interest in their hobbies, you will give a good impression.

The Friend Test might also be the first occasion you have to share your date's attention with another person. Your date and his or her friend(s) are likely going to have things to talk about—some of these will be discussions you can participate in; others might not. Don't feel offended if the conversation veers to a topic you know nothing about, or mutual friends you have never met. Wait until the end of the date to judge how it has gone. If your match recognized these moments and within a reasonable amount of time tried to circle back to a topic you could participate in, then it went fairly well. If your match brings you to this kind of date, then more-or-less ignores you, you might have a problem. How your match treats you in front of his or her friends is just as important as how you treat them. If your match demeans, belittles or in any way insults you in front of his or her friends, you need to think twice about dating that person, no matter how well he or she treats you in private.

» Beyond Friends – Workplaces and Families

Internet dating does not change the process of meeting colleagues, bosses and family. Just because an Internet matching service says you are 90 per cent compatible does not mean that your dad will automatically love your match or that he/she will get along with your brother. It also doesn't mean that he/she will get along with your colleagues or your boss. Internet dating is just a way to meet people—where the relationship goes after that is up to the individuals involved. Since this is still an important area in a relationship, however, I've included a couple of tips for these situations:

» **Introductions to Colleagues and/or your Boss**

Introductions to colleagues are a little trickier than introductions to friends. Office politics exist at even the friendliest of workplaces. Like it or not, boyfriends/girlfriends who display inappropriate behaviour at a work function reflect badly on the worker and in extreme cases can even affect their chances for advancement in the company. What is considered inappropriate behaviour will differ from group to group—the level of decorum expected might differ from a banking firm to a construction firm and the level might also differ depending on the event; whether it is a casual company picnic or a black-tie Christmas party. Always think before you speak/act, dress appropriately for the occasion (save the super sexy stuff for dates rather than work functions) and try to limit your consumption of alcohol so that your judgment isn't impaired, and things will likely go just fine.

In close-knit workplaces where most of the employees are friends there is also a vested interest in the group in looking after one of their own. People will generally be welcoming, but be assured that they will also be assessing you, particularly early on in the relationship. Don't take too much offense at this; they are just trying to look out for their friend and colleague. Once again, all you can do is be yourself but the best-behaving version of yourself, particularly the first couple of times that you meet them.

Just like when you meet your match's friends, pay attention to how your match acts when he/she introduces you to his/her colleagues. If his or her behaviour radically changes, this is not a great sign. People spend as much or more time with their work colleagues as they do with their families, so the dominant culture at their workplace can easily influence their own attitudes and behaviour, even when they are not at work.

» Meeting the Family

The timing of meeting each other's families will have a great deal to do with opportunity. If both halves of the couple live with their parents (i.e. while they attend university) then meeting the families will occur quickly and naturally. If your match's relatives live far away then it can take a lot longer, and may require more formalized planning and effort to make it possible.

In other words, each couple is going to follow a different schedule when it comes meeting each other's relatives, there is no perfect time or magic number of months that will improve/decrease the odds of the relationship being successful.

In the case of my first serious relationship found through Internet dating, both his parents and mine lived in the same city so it was quite easy for both of us to be introduced to each other's family. In our case, however, it happened unusually quickly. We decided to be formal boyfriend/girlfriend in late November and within a month the Christmas holidays provided the opportunity to meet not just each other's parents but most of each other's relatives.

» The Apple Doesn't Fall Far from the Tree – Well, Sometimes

Modern families come in all shapes and sizes, and have many different combinations of beliefs and attitudes (some or all of which your match may or may not share). A good match will warn you in advance of any undercurrents or history that you need to be aware of so that you don't inadvertently step on any toes, start a fight, or come off looking like a fool.

Remember that your match is not his or her family, so don't judge a person too harshly for the way his or her family acts, but pay attention to the way a person acts around family, and how he or she allows his or her family to treat you.

Think long term—if the relationship goes well and eventually you end up married, could you put up with the way the relatives treat you? Be honest with yourself and don't expect the behaviour to change much over time. For example, if your match dismisses all your opinions because they are different than those of his mother or father when his parents are in the room, or if his/her parents or siblings insult you and your match doesn't stand up for you, don't expect this to change just because you marry into the family!

Pay attention to the expectations put on your match by his or her family, as well. Is your match expected to take care of his or her whole family financially? Is he or she expected to be the primary caregiver for his or her parents as they age? Is he or she the main emotional support for his or her mother and/or father? Is it taken for granted that he or she will go over to his/her parents' every weekend to help around the house? Is it a requirement that you have supper with his or her parents every Sunday night? If the relationship is successful and the two of you do end up married, these expectations and responsibilities will likely be extended to both halves of the couple, so make certain that you can accept this role (or at least are able to support your potential spouse in playing this role)!

CHAPTER 11

Relationship Reality

Congratulations! You have succeeded in meeting someone and transitioning from a "match" to being in a relationship. Here are a few final thoughts as you begin this stage of your romantic journey.

» Giving and Receiving Love

There is a great book called *The Five Love Languages*, by Gary D. Chapman which details the five major ways in which people express and receive love. For example, some people need to hear the words in order to feel love while other people may rarely say the words but demonstrate their love through actions. This difference can be likened to one person speaking Greek while the other speaks Mandarin. A couple like this only succeeds if both people become a little "bilingual"—the person who perceived love only through words recognizing that their partner is conveying love through their actions and the person who normally just conveys love through actions learning to convey their feelings verbally a little more often. This book is a great read and one often recommended in marriage prep courses due to its effectiveness in helping couples understand each other and the potential trouble these differences can cause in their relationship over time. Do yourself a favour and read this book.

» When the Going Gets Tough, Beware Temptation

Every real romantic relationship is going to have its ups and downs. It is a fact of life that challenges will come up, sometimes completely out of the blue (from missing your flight to being diagnosed with terminal cancer). Everything can be going fine then suddenly one or the other (or both) people in a relationship can be hit by a sudden stumbling block such as health issue, a layoff, money trouble, a transfer to a different city or a family crisis. Less dramatic, but equally troublesome to a relationship can be the day-to-day stress of work or the burden of trying to make a relationship work with our other time commitments or the monotony of paying bills, doing chores, staying in the same routine, etc. It is almost certain that you and your boyfriend/girlfriend are going to get emotional, have fights, misunderstand each another or unintentionally hurt each other's feelings sooner or later. The key is what you do when faced with these moments.

The downside of Internet dating is that those who have tried it know they have options—stay in their current relationship or go back online to find another match. Many think (even if just for a moment) that ditching a current relationship will solve all their problems, as whatever their romantic partner is faced with wasn't what they signed up for when they got into the relationship. Why should they have to deal with it?

The reality is that those who are genuinely interested in making the relationship work for the long term will put in the effort to be there for each other when the bad or boring times hit, supporting each other however they can. They will apologize when appropriate (even if it takes a few days, and/or some long conversations to explain why they need to apologize in the first place). If they need additional help to deal with their problems (financial counselling, medical help, etc.), they will go out and get it because to them the relationship is worth fighting for.

When the bad times hit or the excitement of the relationship begins to fade, remember what attracted you to your match in the first place, and what has made you put in the time, effort and commitment to stay together until now. If what you really want is for the relationship to succeed, resist the temptation to take the easy route out (breaking up) and do what you can to get through it as a couple. Then, if things don't work out and you do end up breaking up, you can walk away from the relationship with your head held high, secure in the knowledge that you didn't run at the first sign of trouble and you tried your best to deal with whatever life handed you.

» Set Up the Odds in Your Favour

Make resisting temptation easier on yourself by cancelling your Internet dating subscription after you agree to be girlfriend/ boyfriend, or by stopping checking it for matches until the subscription runs out and then cancelling it (most sites keep you on and keep billing you unless you officially terminate your membership). If you keep checking out other options, it is unlikely you are ever going to put the time, effort or hard work necessary to truly connect with your current boyfriend/ girlfriend and make that relationship work.

» Are You Committed to this Relationship or Not?

If you have agreed to be in a relationship but find yourself back on the sites constantly, looking to "upgrade" to a "better" boyfriend/girlfriend, you need to respect the other person enough to tell him or her that you aren't interested having a relationship, break it off, and then go back on the site until you find someone who you will commit to. If you don't, you're just a jackass for stringing your boyfriend/girlfriend along. Even if you don't believe in religion, the universe has a funny way of returning to us all the positive or negative energy we put out, sooner or later.

» Breaking Up Versus Settling for Each Other

Sometimes couples run into situations in which neither has committed any of the other's official deal breakers, but things aren't going so well regardless. Over time, relationships can drift and become so focused on the needs of one person that the needs of the other become lost in the shuffle. This is a trap many women and some men fall into—in order to be a good girlfriend or boyfriend, they stuff down their own feelings and put their own needs entirely aside. In such a case the individual becomes quietly less and less happy as he or she loses himself or herself in the relationship. If this situation continues, the unhappiness will likely be expressed mentally and physically—contributing to depression, anxiety, tension, sexual dysfunction, etc.

I speak from experience on this one, and it is not a lesson I would wish on anyone. Your mind may insist that everything is fine, but if your body is expressing symptoms that seem to have no definitive physical cause, examine all aspects of your life/relationship to see what your body is trying to tell you!

Everyone's life has value and everyone deserves the chance to be happy. If you are suppressing yourself/your feelings to hold on to your relationship, you owe it to yourself to sit down with your romantic partner and talk to him or her about how you feel. Don't blame the other person or try to convince him or her to change, but share your feelings and beliefs. Use specific examples of what behaviour is bothering you and why (e.g.

"When you flirt with other women in front of me, I feel sad, scared and disrespected").

Make it clear that the other person can do whatever he or she wants—but not when the two of you are in a relationship (e.g. "You can date whomever you like, but not when you are with me. If you want to be with me then you have to choose to date only me so long as we are in a relationship." Or "You have the right to choose what you want to do with your time but when I'm in a relationship with someone, if I ask them for help I expect them to choose to help me if they can. Can you do this?").

Make sure to acknowledge and reward any changes that match what you asked for ("I was so impressed tonight; the waitress was really cute but you didn't flirt with her at all. I felt so lucky and proud to be sitting at the table with you;" "Today I was bragging to all my friends about how awesome you are for coming over and helping me fix my fence, put up my pictures, etc.;" "The guys couldn't believe how awesome you were for asking them to come over and watch the games with me after how bad last week was at work, and that you honestly didn't mind the fact we spent all day in front of the TV;" or "Do you have any idea how jealous the guys are knowing I'm going home to an amazing neck massage from a beautiful woman/ man?").

Set a specific time period (e.g. three to six months) during which you will observe to see if they change the behaviour that is bothering you through making them aware of it and rewarding them when they act the way you need. If this period comes to an end and things still haven't improved, it is time to walk away. Don't settle for someone who cannot or will not support you and demonstrate his or her love for you in the way you need to be loved and supported. It is not a reflection on you; it is a reflection on them, their maturity and their choices of how they are living their life.

Another version of settling is when people are in a relationship that they are not happy with but both are afraid to break it off and take their chances on finding relationships that would bring them happiness. They are afraid that they won't find anyone else or that no one else will love them, so they settle for the unsatisfactory relationship as they think it is better than being alone, when in fact it is worse.

Settling for an unsatisfactory relationship means you are constantly trapped in loneliness and constantly without hope. Being single means you are occasionally lonely with the constant hope of finding someone to love who will love you in return.

Don't stay in a bad/unhappy relationship because you are afraid that you will never find someone better or that no one else will ever love you. These statements give away your own self-worth. Is it hard to be on your own? Sometimes. The rewards of living independently and with hope are worth it, however.

» Sealing the Deal – To Marry or Not to Marry?

Deciding whether or not to marry is a very personal choice that only you can make for yourself, but keep a few things in mind. If you put aside all the hoopla of shows like *Rich Bride Poor Bride* and *Say Yes to the Dress,* as well as religious convention and societal expectations, marriage at its heart is two people taking an oath to demonstrate their commitment to each other. Just as we view a doctor's Hippocratic Oath to have more weight than a simple promise, the marriage vows give greater weight to a couple's bond than a simple promise or just living together until they obtain common-law status. Taking these vows can't destroy a good relationship, because nothing about either person or their feelings towards each other will change by saying the words before witnesses, in either a religious or civil ceremony. How each person chooses to act after the words are said will either reinforce your vows, creating a marriage that lasts a lifetime, or break the vows, leading to strife within the marriage and the possibility of divorce as the years go by.

There are also certain legalities around marriage as a civil institution, including visiting rights in the hospital if you get sick, eligibility for a pension/benefits, etc. While living together for a certain amount of time can result in a common-law marriage, official marriage ceremonies can help clarify that you truly want your romantic partner to be part of every aspect of your life and to have all the rights, responsibilities and privileges modern society grants to those who have the status of husband or wife.

Final Thoughts

Keep in mind that Internet dating is just one tool in your dating strategy kit, and the more practice you have, the better you will become at using it. With Internet dating, realistic expectations, proper preparation and perseverance are the keys to setting up the odds of success in your favour, but even these can't guarantee you will meet your romantic partner online. No one can predict where and when you will meet the right person for you, so keep your eyes and mind open to the possibility and increase your odds by pursuing every avenue available to you: Internet dating, singles events, speed dating, participation in hobbies (rowing club, rotary club, etc.), getting set up on dates by friends, etc.

As I continue on my journey of looking for the right romantic partner I wish everyone who is also on this path luck. It is my hope that the tips and advice in this book will make your journey a little smoother than it would have otherwise been, and help you to avoid the mistakes that I and others have made on our journeys looking for love.

> *"The Ultimate Answer to Life, the*
> *Universe and Everything is … 42!"*
> *Deep Thought, The Hitchhiker's Guide to the Galaxy*

Sources

1. *By the Numbers, the Rise of Canada's online Dating scene*, by Staff,
   The Canadian Press, July 15,2015,
   http://globalnews.ca/news/2111560/by-the-numbers-the-rise-of-canadas-online-dating-scene

2. Volume 5, The Sensuality Secrets DVD Collection, Patti Contenta with Guest Speaker Dr. Amir G. Sabongui (www.truelifeskill.com, author of The Art of Social Networking),
   DVD set available at www.sensualitysecrets.com

3. Dr. A. Georges Sabongui, a Psychologist who specializes in inter-personal matters, interviewed in *The Sensuality Secrets* DVD series
   http://www.cliniquealpha.ca/credentials.html
   https://www.sensualitysecrets.com

4. *The 7 Qualities in Men that Women Find Attractive* by Dan Weaver and Rebecca Harrington,
   Business Insider, Dec 24,2016